GROWTH STRATEGY

Omar Mohout

GROWTH STRATEGY

The art of scalable growth

ACADEMIA
PRESS

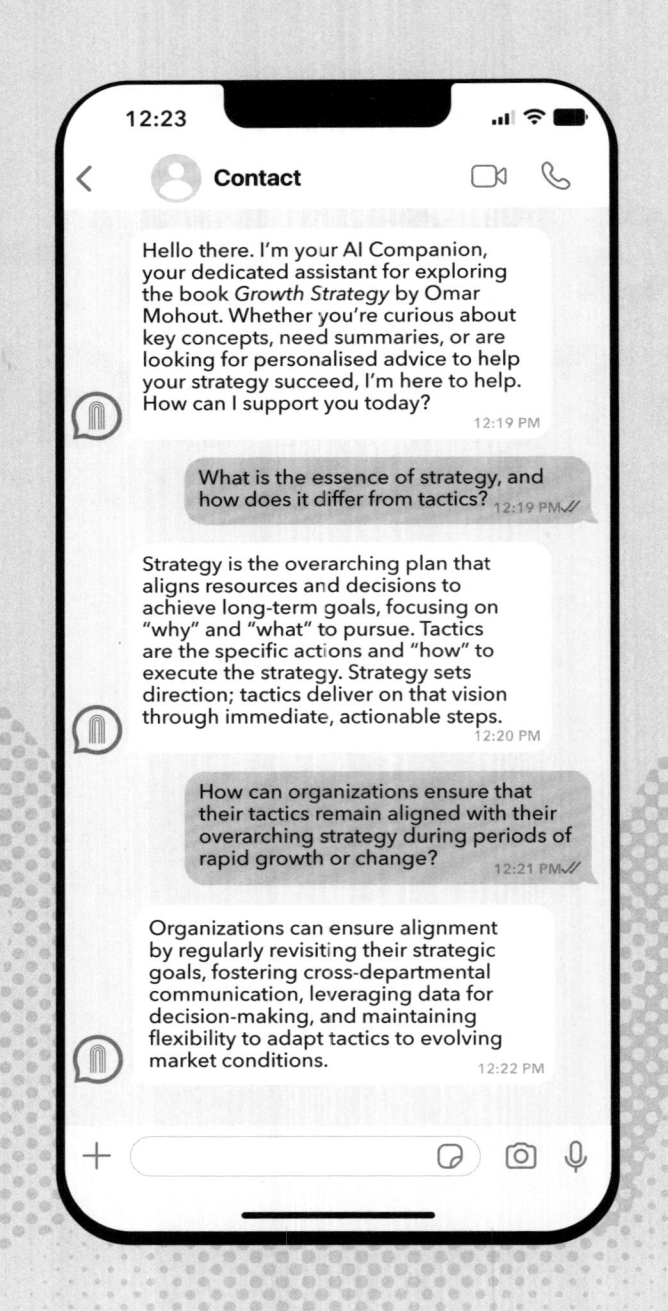

DISCOVER YOUR AI COMPANION

LET'S MAKE THE BOOK ABOUT YOU!

Imagine this: you are not just reading this book, but you are entering into a direct conversation with its contents. It feels like Omar Mohout is sitting right next to you, ready to answer your questions and support you with his knowledge and expertise. On the right, you can see what such a conversation with the AI Companion might look like. The AI Companion tailors the content of *Growth Strategy* perfectly to:

- you as a professional;
- your team;
- your company or organisation;
- and your unique situation.

Through a convenient chat function (available in WhatsApp), you will discover additional features that go beyond the classic learning experience, such as personalised advice, real-time updates and practical tools to apply the insights from the book immediately.

**Experience a new, interactive way of
learning that truly grows with you in three easy steps:**

STEP 1
Go to: **https://click.lannoo.be/ai-growth-strategy**
or scan the QR code on the right and follow the instructions.

STEP 2
To activate the AI Companion, you will need the following unique activation code:

37297fbcd9a6a524

STEP 3
Open the chat and start the conversation.
You get free access from the moment of registration.

CONTENTS

For Aaron,
As you step into your first job and begin this exciting new chapter
of your life, may this book inspire you to approach every challenge
with confidence, every opportunity with curiosity,
and every moment with gratitude. In sha' Allah.

INTRODUCTION

What if everything you thought you knew about growing and scaling a business was wrong? Clearly, there is more to it than simply "working harder." Sometimes, the very things that make a business successful can become obstacles to its growth.

Can you really bottle the magic of expansion? I doubt it. Every business is unique, every market a shifting landscape. But if you are determined to try, this guide might be a good place to start. Inside, you'll find the tools and insights to navigate the complexities of growth and build or expand a business that truly thrives.

In today's competitive market, the harsh reality is that companies failing to achieve critical mass—growing and scaling their operations to become sustainable—will inevitably face failure, regardless of the quality of their product or solution. Simply creating value isn't sufficient for success; that value must be effectively distributed to a broad audience. A top-tier product can still falter if the company lacks the necessary reach and market penetration. Growth and scalability are critical because they ensure that a business can not only attract but also retain a substantial customer base, expand its market share, and continuously generate revenue at a scale that supports its operations and ambitions. Without this expansion, even the most innovative and potentially transformative products risk fading into obscurity, unable to sustain the business long-term. Thus, the ability to scale and distribute value broadly is just as crucial as the value creation itself. In other words, you need a growth strategy to realize the full potential of a business model. And for the record, copy-pasting someone else's growth strategy doesn't work because the voice that suits them doesn't necessarily suit you, even if they have the same business model.

Expanding a business seamlessly intertwines elements of both art and science. It demands not only a profound grasp of strategic nuances but also a meticulous attention to detail and an unwavering commitment to continuous improvement. In this expanded guide, I aim to dissect and discuss the diverse and dynamic approaches to growth strategies. Drawing from a broad spectrum of industries and leveraging established best practices, I intend to equip business leaders with actionable insights and tools. My objective is to serve as a practical resource for those at the helm of navigating the intricate journey of business growth and scaling efforts. Every company is unique and so is its expansion process. However, the best way to prepare for what is ahead is to learn from fellow entrepreneurs who have already paved the way. I hope this publication contributes to this exchange of best practices and lessons learned.

This guide has been carefully structured to act as a detailed manual on the art of business expansion. Each chapter meticulously explores essential facets of growth and scaling, infused with practical advice, strategic frameworks, and illustrative examples from the real world. But that's not all. This book also provides an AI-supported application to transform your business expansion into a successful and sustainable growth strategy. Through the combination of insights, practical examples, and AI support, this book is a complete guide for those who want to understand growth strategy and apply it successfully. With the **AI Companion**, you will experience an interactive way of learning that grows with you. Throughout the book, we regularly give you suggestions of questions to ask. Tailored to business executives, budding entrepreneurs, and all those charged with spearheading growth initiatives within their organizations, this handbook aims to foster a comprehensive understanding of the processes involved in devising, deploying, and refining effective growth strategies. By the end of this book, readers will have a robust understanding of how to formulate, implement, and optimize growth strategies.

Acknowledgments

My heartfelt appreciation goes out to the myriad of experts, scaleups, multinationals and institutions whose contributions have been pivotal in shaping this guide. I am particularly grateful to Beatrice De Keyzer, who was the sounding board that shaped this final result, and to my former colleagues at Nova Reperta, specifically Jan Verdonck. My thanks also extend to VOKA (the Flemish network of entrepreneurs) and the Solvay Brussels School of Economics & Management, who have provided numerous opportunities through workshops focused on the exploration and mastery of growth and scaling strategies over the years. These experiences have been instrumental in enriching the content and depth of this book, enabling me to offer a richer, more comprehensive guide.

Growth is not merely a goal; it's a mindset, a problem-solving tool, and a compass that guides our journey toward a successful and fulfilling future. By embracing these principles and focusing on key areas of growth, we can achieve our aspirations and create a thriving business that delivers value to our customers, our employees, and our stakeholders.

GUIDING PRINCIPLES

GROWTH = MINDSET
Cultivate a growth mindset that embraces innovation, experimentation, and continuous improvement

GROWTH = PROBLEM SOLVER
View growth as a solution to challenges, enabling us to overcome obstacles and achieve our goals

GROWTH = COMPASS
Utilize growth as a guiding principle, directing our decisions and actions toward a clear vision of the future

GROWTH = VALUE CREATION
Focus on creating value for our customers, employees, and stakeholders

GROWTH = SUSTAINABILITY

CHAPTER

1

UNDER STANDING GROWTH STRATEGY

Growth is messy, as any parent can tell you.

What is strategy?

Before we dive into the specifics of growth strategy, let's take a step back and explore the very essence of strategy itself.

Imagine a ship setting sail. It's not enough to simply have a powerful engine and a skilled crew. To reach its destination, the ship needs a charted course, a clear direction that guides its journey through unpredictable waters. That's what strategy provides—a deliberate path toward a desired outcome.

At its core, strategy can be thought of as the comprehensive set of actions and decisions an organization adopts to achieve its long-term goals. However, this simplistic definition only scratches the surface. To delve deeper, strategy encompasses the deliberate planning and allocation of resources to carve out a competitive advantage. This advantage is often anchored in a unique value proposition that differentiates the organization within its specific field or industry.

Strategy transcends mere short-term tactics by embedding itself in the broader vision and trajectory of the organization. It is not just about choosing what to do, but also about deciding what not to pursue. A well-crafted strategy acts as a dynamic roadmap, navigating the organization through both predictable challenges and unforeseen opportunities. It ensures that every tactical decision and action is coherent and synchronizes with the overarching objectives of the enterprise.

In a world of limited time and resources, strategy helps you prioritize and make the most impactful decisions.

Key elements of strategy

- **Defining your destination:** where do you want to be? A clear vision of your goals is essential for creating a strategy to achieve them.
- **Understanding your current position:** where are you now? An honest assessment of your strengths, weaknesses, and current market conditions is crucial for charting a realistic course.
- **Mapping the terrain:** what challenges and opportunities lie ahead? Analyzing your competitive landscape, industry trends, and potential risks will help you navigate the journey.
- **Plotting the course:** how will you get from where you are to where you want to be? This involves identifying key initiatives, allocating resources, and setting milestones.

- **Adapting to the journey:** the sea is rarely calm. A good strategy is flexible and adaptable, allowing you to adjust your course in response to unexpected events and new information.

Strategy vs. tactics

It's important to distinguish between strategy and tactics.

- **Strategy** is the overarching plan, the "why" behind your actions. It's about making choices that align with your long-term goals.
- **Tactics** are the specific actions you take to implement your strategy, the "how" of achieving your objectives.

Think of it this way: strategy is deciding how to win the war, while tactics are the individual battles fought along the way.

Why is strategy important?

In today's complex and competitive business environment, a well-defined strategy is more critical than ever. It helps you:

- **Focus your efforts:** by prioritizing key initiatives, you avoid spreading yourself too thin and instead maximize your impact.
- **Gain a competitive advantage:** a strong strategy allows you to differentiate yourself and outmaneuver potential rivals.
- **Allocate resources effectively:** by aligning your resources with your strategic goals, you ensure that every investment contributes to your overall success.
- **Navigate uncertainty:** a flexible strategy helps you adapt to changing market conditions and unexpected challenges.

- **Drive organizational alignment:** a shared understanding of the strategy ensures that everyone in the company is working toward the same goals.

The foundation for growth

A solid understanding of strategy is the foundation for developing an effective growth strategy. In the next chapter, we will explore how to apply these principles to the specific challenge of expanding your business.

What is growth strategy?

Forget the buzzwords and complex frameworks for a moment. At its core, a growth strategy is simply a plan to achieve sustainable expansion. An organization's plan for overcoming current and future challenges to realize its goals for expansion. A roadmap that guides your business toward a larger, more impactful future. You are right, every strategy inherently contributes to growth in some way. Whether it's optimizing operations, enhancing customer experience, or innovating new products, the ultimate goal is to move the needle forward. But a dedicated growth strategy provides a focused framework for these efforts, aligning your entire organization around a common vision for expansion.

In essence, a robust growth strategy is pivotal for any organization seeking to maintain relevance and achieve sustained success. It enables businesses to leverage their unique strengths, meet the evolving needs of their customers, and continuously adapt to the shifting landscapes of their industries.

For startups, growth strategies are the ignition switch, sparking the initial burst of momentum that propels them along the "S-curve" of company growth. It's about finding product-market fit, acquiring early customers, and establishing a foothold in the market. But for mature companies, growth strategies take on a different form. They become the escape velocity needed to break free from the gravitational pull of the plateau, to overcome the inertia of stagnation and reach the next orbit of expansion. Basically, what brought them to this level will not necessarily bring them to the next. It's about reinvention, diversification, and a relentless pursuit of new horizons.

Why focus on growth?

In the dynamic world of business, standing still is akin to moving backward. A well-defined growth strategy is essential for:

- **Increasing revenue and profitability:** this is the most obvious goal, achieved by expanding your customer base, increasing sales, and optimizing pricing.
- **Gaining market share:** outpacing your competitors and capturing a larger slice of the market strengthens your position and influence.
- **Building brand equity:** growth often leads to increased visibility and recognition, enhancing your brand's value and reputation.
- **Attracting and retaining talent:** a company with a clear growth trajectory is more appealing to ambitious employees, fostering a motivated and engaged workforce.

- **Ensuring long-term sustainability:** growth allows you to adapt to changing market conditions, invest in innovation, and secure your future in a competitive landscape.

Beyond the bottom line

While financial performance is a key indicator of success, growth strategies can also encompass broader goals. While growth strategies ultimately aim to boost a company's top line (revenue) and/or bottom line (profit), they represent a diverse set of approaches with varying objectives. Some strategies prioritize expanding **market share**, capturing a larger slice of the pie and solidifying market dominance. Others focus on **maximizing company value**, aiming for long-term profitability and sustainability that attracts investors, drives up stock prices, and facilitates attractive liquidity events such as an exit. Some growth strategies prioritize **user acquisition**, aiming to build a large and engaged customer base, particularly crucial in today's digital landscape and essential for freemium-based business models. Increasingly, companies are also incorporating **social impact** into their growth strategies, recognizing that positive contributions to society and the environment can drive customer loyalty and enhance brand reputation. Lastly, **cash flow**—keeping your company afloat—could be the priority.

Figure 1 • What kind of growth are we talking about?

However, it's crucial to remember that these diverse objectives ultimately feed back into the fundamental drivers of business success: increased revenue and profitability. Whether it's through gaining market share, enhancing company value, or building a loyal user base, a successful growth strategy must inevitably translate into a stronger top and bottom line, sooner rather than later.

Downscaling

While the pursuit of growth is often seen as the holy grail of business, there is a counterintuitive strategy that can be equally powerful: downscaling. This involves intentionally reducing the size and scope of your business, streamlining operations, closing underperforming (international) branches, and focusing on core strengths. It might seem counterintuitive, but in certain situations downscaling can be the key to achieving long-term sustainability and even renewed growth.

Downscaling is not about admitting defeat; it's about making strategic choices to ensure the long-term health of your business. Here are some common reasons why companies choose to downscale:

- **Refocusing on core competencies:** by shedding non-essential activities, businesses can concentrate resources on what they do best, improving efficiency and competitiveness.
- **Adapting to changing market conditions:** when faced with declining demand, increased competition, or economic downturns, downscaling can help businesses weather the storm and emerge stronger.
- **Improving profitability:** by reducing overhead costs and streamlining operations, companies can boost profitability even with lower revenue.
- **Reducing complexity:** downscaling can simplify operations and improve decision-making.

It's important to distinguish between two types of downscaling: strategic and distress downscaling. The first is a proactive, planned approach to resizing the business, driven by a desire to improve efficiency, focus on core strengths, or adapt to changing market conditions. The latter is a reactive response to financial difficulties or declining performance, often involving layoffs, asset sales, and other drastic measures. Downscaling is not simply about cutting costs; it requires a strategic approach to ensure a smooth transition and minimize disruption. Paradoxically, downscaling can sometimes be a catalyst for future growth. By streamlining operations, refocusing on core strengths, and improving profitability, businesses can create a solid foundation for future expansion. Downscaling is a powerful strategic tool that can help businesses navigate challenging times, improve efficiency, and position themselves for future success. **While it may seem counterintuitive, knowing when to scale *down* is just as important as knowing when to scale *up*.** By embracing the strategic power of downscaling, businesses can ensure their long-term sustainability and thrive in an ever-changing world.

While it may seem counterintuitive,
knowing when to scale down
is just as important as knowing
when to grow.

<u>Explanation</u>

Top line: the "top line" of a business refers to its gross sales or revenue. This is the total amount of money a business brings in from its usual business activities, like selling goods or services, before any expenses are subtracted. When people talk about a company's top line, they are looking at how effective it is at generating sales and bringing money in, not necessarily at how much profit it's making after all the expenses are subtracted. This number is typically found at the top of a company's income statement, which is why it's called the top line.

Bottom line: the "bottom line" of a business refers to its net income or profit, which is the amount of money that remains after all expenses, taxes, and additional income streams are subtracted. This figure tells you how much the company actually earned or lost during a specific period. It's called the bottom line because it appears at the bottom of an income statement, summarizing the final financial state of the company after all financial transactions have been considered. Essentially, the bottom line shows how effective a company is at converting its revenue into profit, making it a crucial indicator of the company's financial health and efficiency.

Unique value proposition: this is a clear statement that explains how your product solves customers' problems or improves their situation, what benefits customers can expect, and why customers should buy from you over your competitors.

Why growth is non-negotiable

The big why for having a growth strategy? In essence, growth has one—and only one—true purpose: making an organization sustainable. Not just surviving for another quarter or another year, but truly thriving in the face of ever-changing market dynamics, disruptive technologies, and evolving customer expectations. Think of a tree extending its roots deeper and wider, not just to stand taller but to withstand storms, access vital nutrients, and support the flourishing ecosystem it sustains. A well-crafted growth strategy provides that same resilience, ensuring your business remains relevant, adaptable, and competitive for years to come. It's about building a business that not only survives but also flourishes, leaving a lasting legacy. A growth strategy provides the framework for achieving that long-term vision and resilience, guiding your decisions and actions toward a future where your organization continues to create value and make a positive impact instead of chasing fleeting gains.

But sustainable growth requires more than just an upward trajectory on a chart. It demands a clear sense of purpose, a guiding principle that shapes the how and why of expansion. What value are you creating through your growth? How does it benefit your customers, your employees, and the wider community? Growth for the sake of growth, without a clear objective or meaningful contribution, can be as destructive as stagnation. Like a cancer, it can consume resources, distort priorities, and ultimately weaken the very foundation of the organization, leaving it vulnerable to collapse. Purposeful growth, on the other hand, strengthens the core, fuels innovation, and creates lasting value for all stakeholders.

SUSTAINABILITY

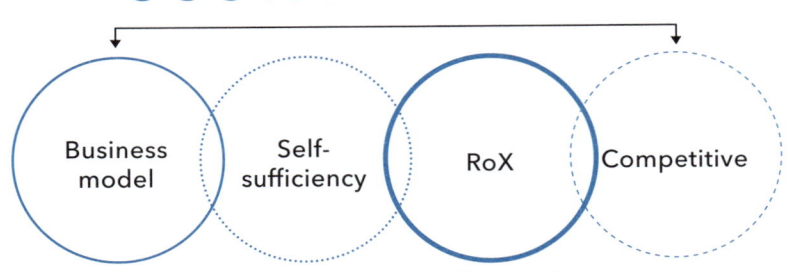

Figure 2 • Key elements of sustainability

To achieve true sustainability, we need to consider four interconnected elements, visualized as pillars supporting the overall structure.

Business model: a sustainable business model is built on a solid foundation of value creation. It clearly defines how the company delivers value to its customers, generates revenue, and maintains profitability over the long term. This pillar ensures that the business remains financially viable and capable of supporting its growth ambitions. Crucially, the business model also determines the critical mass necessary for sustainability. For instance, a coffee bar in a bustling city might need just 250 customers per day to become sustainable, while a technology company building a mobile app might need 2,000,000 users to achieve the same level of viability. Understanding this critical mass is essential for setting realistic growth targets and aligning your strategy with your business model. Furthermore, it's crucial to have a clear vision of the desired magnitude of your business. Are you aiming for a local business with a loyal customer base of hundreds? Or a global enterprise serving millions? Thinking in terms of orders of magnitude—10,

100, 1,000, 100,000, or even 1,000,000,000 customers, employees, or units of revenue—helps you grasp the scale you need to attain. This "endgame" thinking provides a crucial framework for planning and resource allocation. By envisioning the future size and scope of your business, you can better estimate the resources, funding, and infrastructure required to reach that level of sustainability. This is a crucial point that often gets overlooked in discussions about growth. **Understanding the desired scale of your business is essential for effective planning and resource allocation.**

Self-sufficiency: a sustainable business, especially in the context of growth, must strive for financial self-sufficiency. While it's common to rely on external funding sources like venture capital or loans to fuel initial expansion, a truly sustainable business ultimately generates enough revenue to cover its operational costs, finance future growth, invest in innovation, and repay its debts. This internal financial strength provides a crucial buffer against economic downturns, market fluctuations, and unforeseen challenges. Remember, the most common cause of business failure is cash flow problems—the inability to pay bills and salaries. Obviously, gains from business expansion must offset the associated costs. Achieving financial self-sufficiency ensures the company has the resources to weather storms, seize opportunities, and continue its growth trajectory without constantly relying on external lifelines. It's about building a robust financial engine that powers the business forward. As Warren Buffett famously said, "Only when the tide goes out do you discover who's been swimming naked." When economic conditions take a turn for the worse, it's the financially self-sufficient businesses that are able to withstand the currents and emerge stronger.

RoX: this represents the driving force behind the business, the passion and purpose that motivates its leaders and employees. Every business has an "I," as in ROI—the return on investment that drives financial decisions. But sustainable growth is fueled by something more, something that transcends purely financial gains. This is the X factor, the intrinsic motivation that inspires individuals to go above and beyond, to pour their heart and soul into the company's mission. It's the "why" that goes beyond profit, encompassing the desire to make a difference, create something meaningful, or leave a positive impact on the world. While the "I" can bring you initial success, it can only take you so far. To truly achieve sustainable growth, you need the "X"—that burning passion, that unwavering belief in your mission, that shared sense of purpose that unites and inspires your team. As Antoine de Saint-Exupéry wisely said, "If you want to build a ship, don't drum up the men to gather wood, divide the work and give orders. Instead, teach them to yearn for the vast and endless sea." In other words, ignite their passion for the journey, not just the destination.

Competitive landscape: a sustainable business understands that it doesn't exist in a vacuum. You are not alone in the market, and your growth strategy will inevitably be shaped by the competitive forces surrounding you. This means recognizing that you'll be compelled to take a position—a space you occupy in the market—and that position will inherently dictate your size and scope. Are you the cost leader, the innovator, the niche specialist, or the challenger to the status quo? Your competitive positioning influences every aspect of your growth strategy, from product development and marketing to pricing and distribution. In today's rapidly evolving markets, where the speed of change is accelerating, this outside-in perspective is crucial. Constantly monitoring the competitive landscape allows you to identify emerging trends, anticipate threats, and seize opportunities. Competition can be a powerful driver of innovation, forcing you to differentiate yourself and constantly improve your offerings. But it can also be an opportunity to explore different avenues of growth. Perhaps there is a niche market underserved by larger players, or maybe strategic partnerships or acquisitions can propel you to a new level. For businesses with venture capital or private equity on board, competition is an exit opportunity, the reason why they invested in you in the first place. Competition doesn't always have to be a zero-sum game. Furthermore, competition can also be a foundation for collaboration. By identifying areas of shared interest or complementary strengths, businesses can form strategic partnerships that create synergies and expand their reach. This can lead to the development of entire ecosystems, where companies cooperate to deliver comprehensive solutions and create value for all stakeholders. In this sense, competition can be a catalyst not just for individual growth, but also for the collective evolution of an entire industry. Competition, both new and old, acts as a compass for growth, guiding you toward opportunities, revealing potential threats, and inviting you to constantly reassess your position in the ever-evolving market.

By strengthening each of these pillars, businesses can create a solid foundation for sustainable growth, ensuring their long-term success and resilience in a constantly evolving world. **Growth is a means to organizational value, and that value is expressed as sustainability.** When you grow, everything else tends to fall into place.

While the Playing to Win framework (see chapter 2) offers valuable guidance for strategic decision-making, it has also faced some criticism. Some argue that the framework is overly simplistic and doesn't adequately address the complexities of today's dynamic business environment. Others point out that the focus on winning can lead to an overly competitive mindset, potentially neglecting opportunities for collaboration and partnership. Additionally, the framework's emphasis on deliberate choice and analysis may not be suitable for all situations, particularly in fast-moving markets where agility and rapid adaptation are crucial. Despite these criticisms, Playing to Win remains a valuable resource for strategic thinking, providing a clear and concise framework for making critical choices about where to compete and how to achieve sustainable success.

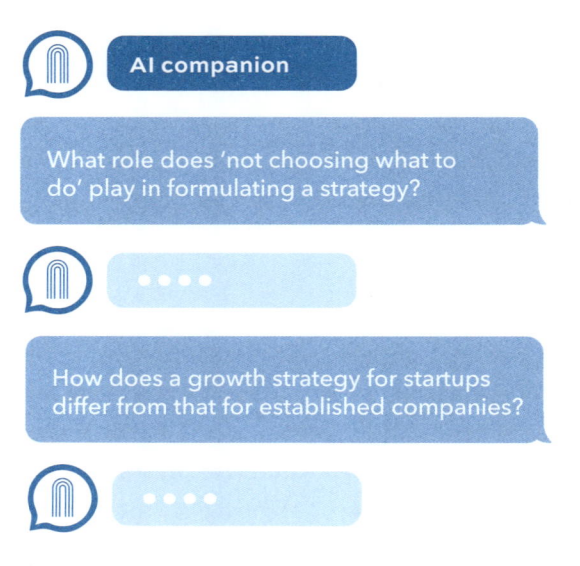

CHAPTER
2

DUAL ENGINES OF GROWTH: EXPANDING OUTWARD AND GROWING FROM WITHIN

"Once you start thinking about growth, it's hard to think about anything else." **Bob Lucas**

Where to play, how to win: mapping your growth territory

Imagine a general preparing for battle. Victory depends not only on the strength of their army but also on choosing the right battlefield and employing the right tactics. Similarly, in the realm of business, a successful growth strategy hinges on two critical decisions: where to play and how to win. This powerful concept, popularized in the influential book *Playing to Win* by A.G. Lafley and Roger Martin, provides a framework for making strategic choices that drive sustainable growth. They argue that a winning strategy is essentially the answer to six fundamental questions, and by thoughtfully addressing these questions, you can chart a course for achieving sustainable competitive advantage and driving meaningful growth.

The first two questions—"What is your winning aspiration?" and "Where will you play?"—help define your competitive arena. Your winning aspiration articulates the ambitious goal you aim to achieve—the ultimate destination of your growth journey. "Where to play" then clarifies the specific battlefield where you'll pursue this aspiration. It involves making deliberate choices about which markets to enter, which customer segments to target, and which products or services to offer. This decision requires a deep understanding of your external environment, carefully analyzing factors like market size, growth potential, profitability, and competitive intensity. But it's not just about finding an attractive market; it's also about identifying where your unique strengths and capabilities give you a right to win. Crucially, the chosen playing field must align with your overall aspirations, values, and available resources.

The next three questions—"What is your product?", "Who is your customer?", and "What is the value proposition for this customer?"—delve into the core of your offering and how it creates value in your chosen arena. Defining your product goes beyond its physical attributes or features; it encompasses the entire customer experience, including service, branding, and delivery. Identifying your ideal customer requires a deep understanding of their needs, motivations, and aspirations. And articulating your value proposition clarifies how your product uniquely addresses those needs and provides superior value compared to the competition.

Finally, the question "How will you win against your competition?" addresses your competitive advantage—the unique capabilities or resources that enable you to outperform rivals in your chosen arena. Will you achieve this through operational excellence, delivering products or services with greater efficiency and reliability than your rivals? Or will you focus on customer intimacy, building deep relationships and tailoring your offerings to their specific needs? Perhaps you'll pursue product leadership, continuously innovating and pushing the boundaries of what is possible. The choice of "how to win" must be carefully aligned with your "where to play" decision, creating a cohesive and powerful strategy.

By thoughtfully and deliberately answering these six questions, as advocated in *Playing to Win*, you can create a focused and effective growth strategy. This framework provides a powerful tool for making strategic choices, allocating resources effectively, and achieving sustainable success in the marketplace. It's about choosing your battles wisely and developing a winning game plan.

A successful growth strategy
addresses **six fundamental questions**:

1 What is your winning aspiration?

2 What is your product?

3 Where is your market?

4 Who is your customer?

5 What is the value proposition for this customer?

6 How will you win against your competition?

Determining where to play involves identifying the markets and segments that offer the best opportunities for growth. It's about understanding the competitive landscape and positioning your business to capture market share. How to win focuses on the actions and capabilities needed to succeed in these chosen markets.

Useful frameworks include the popular Ansoff Matrix and the Blue Ocean Strategy. The Ansoff Matrix guides decisions on market penetration, product development, market development, and diversification. For instance, Starbucks uses market development to enter new geographic regions and product development to introduce new offerings like the Starbucks Reserve line. The Blue Ocean Strategy focuses on creating new market space (blue oceans) rather than competing in existing markets (red oceans). Cirque du Soleil created a new market by combining circus arts with theater, avoiding competition with traditional circuses.

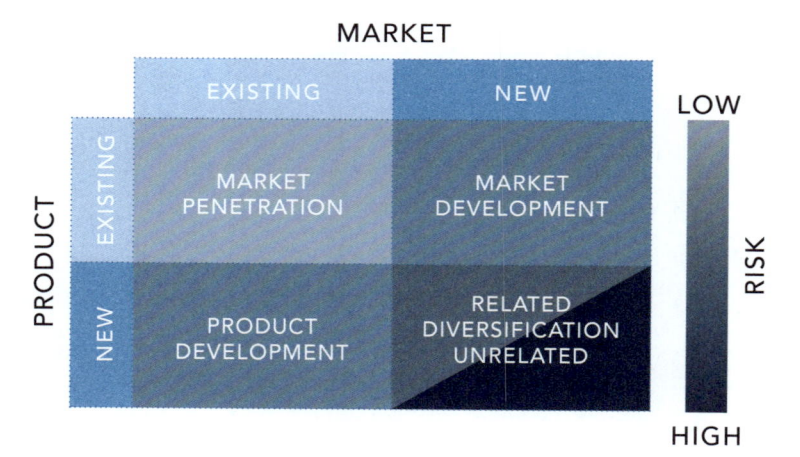

Figure 3 • Ansoff matrix

Profit from the core: unlocking growth from within

While the quest for new markets and customers often dominates growth strategies, there is a powerful alternative that often gets overlooked: **growing from within.** This approach, championed in Chris Zook and James Allen's insightful book *Profit from the Core*, emphasizes the untapped potential within a company's existing customer base and core business.

Profit from the Core challenges the prevailing notion that growth must always come from external expansion. Instead, it advocates for a "back to basics" approach, urging businesses to refocus on their core strengths and deepen their relationships with existing customers. This strategy is particularly relevant in turbulent times, when venturing into uncharted territory can be risky and resource-intensive.

The book highlights several compelling reasons to prioritize growth from within:

- **Increased profitability:** acquiring new customers is typically more expensive than retaining existing ones. By focusing on serving your core customer base better, you can increase their lifetime value and boost profitability.
- **Reduced risk:** expanding into new markets or launching new products carries inherent risks. Growth from within leverages existing strengths and knowledge, minimizing uncertainty and increasing the likelihood of success.
- **Enhanced customer loyalty:** by deepening relationships with existing customers and exceeding their expectations, you can

build strong loyalty and advocacy, creating a sustainable competitive advantage.

- **Improved efficiency:** focusing on your core business allows you to streamline operations, optimize processes, and leverage existing resources more effectively.

Profit from the Core provides a practical framework for achieving growth from within:

1. **Define your core:** clearly identify your core business, your core customers, and your core competencies. What do you do best? Who are your most valuable customers?

2. **Maximize core profitability:** optimize your core business to achieve maximum profitability. This could involve improving operational efficiency, enhancing customer service, or developing new offerings that resonate with your core customers.

3. **Expand concentrically:** once you have maximized your core, explore opportunities to expand concentrically into adjacent markets or product lines that leverage your existing strengths and customer relationships.

4. **Build a repeatable model:** develop a systematic approach to identifying and exploiting growth opportunities within your core, creating a sustainable engine for long-term growth.

This "profit from the core" strategy offers a compelling alternative to the relentless pursuit of external growth. It encourages businesses to look inward, to nurture their existing customer relationships, and to unlock the hidden potential within their core business. In a world of constant change and uncertainty, this focus on internal strength and customer loyalty can provide a stable foundation for sustainable growth.

While the "profit from the core" strategy offers a compelling alternative to relentless external expansion, it also has its limitations. Critics argue that an excessive focus on the core can lead to missed opportunities in emerging markets or new technologies. Additionally, the strategy may not be suitable for businesses in rapidly evolving industries where innovation and disruption are constant forces. Furthermore, defining the "core" can be challenging, particularly for diversified companies with multiple business units. Despite these limitations, this strategy provides valuable insights into the importance of leveraging existing strengths and customer relationships to drive sustainable growth, especially in times of uncertainty.

By acknowledging these limitations and criticisms, you provide a more balanced perspective and encourage readers to critically evaluate the applicability of these frameworks to their specific situations. This fosters a more nuanced understanding of strategic thinking and promotes a more informed approach to growth strategy development.

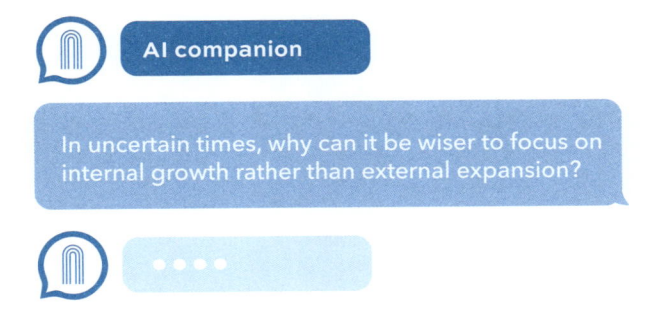

AI companion

In uncertain times, why can it be wiser to focus on internal growth rather than external expansion?

CHAPTER

3

DEFINING WINNING ASPIRATIONS

Growth isn't a strategy—it's a result.

Setting the ambition level

Winning aspirations are the North Star that guides an organization's growth journey. They are the long-term goals, the ambitious visions of the future that fuel passion, inspire action, and provide a clear sense of direction. They define what success ultimately looks like, going beyond mere financial targets to encompass broader ambitions for market leadership, customer impact, or even societal change. By clearly articulating these aspirations, businesses can align their efforts, resources, and decision-making toward achieving a common vision, fostering a sense of shared purpose that propels them forward.

Think of winning aspirations as the engine of growth. They provide the driving force that pushes a company to innovate, expand, and constantly strive for better. Without a clear aspiration, growth can become aimless, lacking the focus and intensity needed to achieve breakthrough success. A well-defined aspiration, on the other hand, acts as a powerful magnet, attracting talent, resources, and opportunities that align with the company's vision.

Examples of winning aspirations might include "moonshots" that truly capture the spirit of ambitious growth:

- **Revolutionizing an entire industry:** this could involve disrupting the status quo with a groundbreaking innovation, creating a new market category, or fundamentally changing the way business is done in a particular sector. Think of companies like Tesla revolutionizing the automotive industry with electric vehicles, or Airbnb transforming the hospitality sector.
- **Solving a global challenge:** this could involve developing solutions to pressing global issues like climate change, poverty, or disease. Imagine a company aiming to provide clean energy to every household on the planet or eradicate a major disease through innovative medical technology.
- **Achieving a seemingly impossible technological breakthrough:** this could involve pushing the boundaries of science and technology to achieve what was once considered impossible. Think of companies like SpaceX aiming to colonize Mars, or researchers working to cure previously incurable diseases.
- **Creating a product or service that fundamentally changes people's lives:** this could involve developing a product or service that dramatically improves people's quality of life, empowers them in new ways, or connects them on a deeper level. Imagine a company creating technology that enables instant communication across any language barrier, or a service that provides personalized education to every child in the world.

- **Building a company that lasts for centuries:** this involves creating a legacy that extends far beyond the current generation, building a company that continues to thrive and make a positive impact for centuries to come. Think of companies like Disney, with its enduring legacy of entertainment and storytelling.

These "moonshot" aspirations represent bold visions of the future, inspiring companies to push their boundaries, pursue ambitious goals, and make a lasting impact on the world.

For most of us, however, our aspirations might be more mundane yet no less important for driving growth and achieving success. This might involve becoming the market leader in a specific industry, achieving a significant revenue or profitability milestone, or creating a meaningful social impact within our community. Whether it's reaching a specific financial target, establishing dominance in a niche market, or developing a product that improves people's lives, these aspirations provide the fuel and direction for our growth journey.

By setting and pursuing winning aspirations, whether it's a "moonshot" or a more grounded goal, companies can unlock their growth potential, driving innovation, attracting talent, and achieving remarkable milestones on their journey to success.

Google's aspiration to "organize the world's information and make it universally accessible and useful"[1] is a prime example of a winning aspiration that fuels growth. This ambitious vision has guided Google's innovation and product development, leading to the creation of

---

1   https://www.google.com/intl/en/search/howsearchworks/our-approach/

groundbreaking products like Google Search, Google Maps, and Google Scholar, all of which align with their overarching goal. This aspiration not only provides a clear direction for growth but also fosters a culture of innovation and a commitment to making a positive impact on the world.

Similarly, the concept of a Big Hairy Audacious Goal (BHAG), coined by Jim Collins and Jerry Porras in their book *Built to Last*, exemplifies a long-term, ambitious goal that galvanizes and unites an organization toward a common vision. A BHAG is ambitious, often stretching the boundaries of what seems possible. It's a goal that is externally questionable but internally regarded as achievable, inspiring employees to strive for extraordinary accomplishments.

A well-known example of a BHAG is SpaceX's goal to make human life multi-planetary by establishing a self-sustaining colony on Mars. This audacious goal, ambitious in its scope and timeline, reflects a bold vision that goes beyond incremental progress and aims for transformative impact. By setting such a lofty objective, SpaceX has aligned its resources, innovation efforts, and organizational culture toward making space travel more accessible and sustainable. This BHAG serves as a powerful catalyst for growth, driving significant advancements and inspiring remarkable milestones in the pursuit of a truly extraordinary vision.

By setting and pursuing winning aspirations, whether it's through a clearly defined vision or a BHAG, companies can unlock their growth potential, driving innovation, attracting talent, and achieving remarkable milestones on their journey to success.

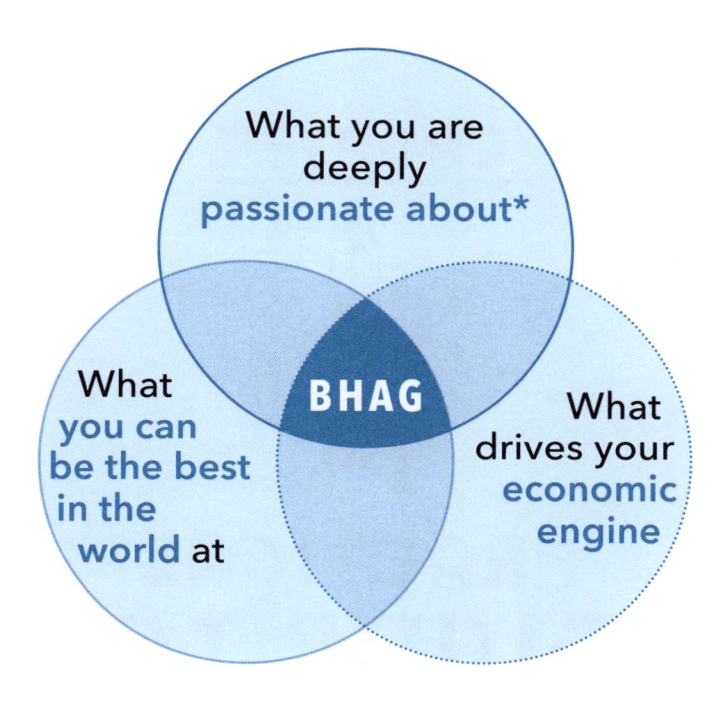

* This includes your core values and purpose

Figure 4 • The concept of Big Hairy Audacious Goals (BHAG)

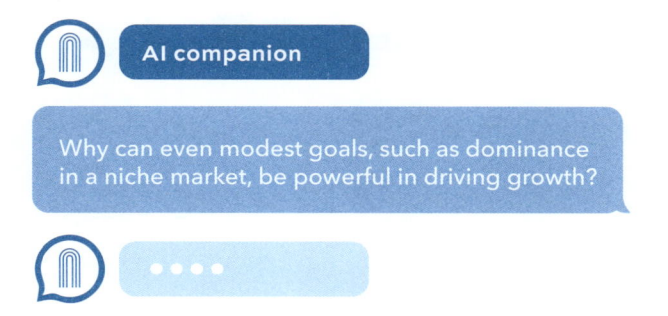

AI companion

Why can even modest goals, such as dominance in a niche market, be powerful in driving growth?

CHAPTER 4

A PRACTICAL GUIDE TO QUANTIFYING GROWTH

"Growth is never by mere chance; it is the result of forces working together." **James Cash Penney**

While aspirations and strategic frameworks provide a compass for your growth journey, it's crucial to translate those ambitions into tangible metrics and measurable goals. This chapter delves into the art of quantifying growth, exploring Key Performance Indicators (KPIs), benchmarks, and rules of thumb that can help you track progress, identify areas for improvement, and make informed decisions along the way.

Compound annual growth rate (CAGR)

One useful way to quantify growth is by looking at the Compound Annual Growth Rate (CAGR), specifically over a sustained period. Imagine you plant a tree. In the first year, it grows 5 inches. The next year, it grows another 6 inches. But it's not just growing from the original height; it's also growing on top of the previous year's growth. That's the idea behind CAGR. It measures the average annual growth rate over a specific period, taking into account this compounding effect. CAGR smooths out the bumps of uneven growth over the years and gives you a single, consistent number to represent your overall growth trajectory. This makes it easier to compare your growth performance over different periods or against other companies.

The formula looks complex but spreadsheets offer a built-in function for calculation:

$$CAGR\ (\%) = \frac{Ending\ Value\ (1 \div t)}{Beginning\ Value} - 1$$

The OECD (a club of mostly rich countries, as *The Economist* would say)[2] provides a helpful framework for categorizing CAGR, with the caveat that these growth rates must be sustained for at least three consecutive years to be considered valid:

- **Growth:** CAGR < 10% (for 3+ years)
  This represents steady, gradual growth. Even 1% growth can be a significant achievement, especially if a market or industry is contracting. This type of growth often focuses on stability, efficiency, and maintaining market share in challenging conditions.

---

2   https://www.economist.com/the-economist-explains/2017/07/05/what-is-the-oecd

- **Fast growth:** 10% ≤ CAGR ≤ 40% (for 3+ years)
  This signifies a more rapid expansion phase and arguably the sweet spot for many companies and organizations. Double-digit growth rates are generally favored by shareholders and indicate a healthy trajectory for scaling the business, increasing market share, and generating strong returns.
- **Hypergrowth:** CAGR > 40% (for 3+ years)
  This indicates exceptionally fast growth, often seen in startups or companies disrupting their industries. Hypergrowth is rare. Achieving hypergrowth is generally easier when starting from a smaller base, as the relative impact of each new customer or sale is greater. For larger, established companies, sustaining hypergrowth often requires significant innovation, strategic acquisitions, or tapping into new markets.

These benchmarks, applied to revenue, profits, or employee count, provide a useful yardstick for businesses to assess their growth performance relative to broader economic trends.

Triple, Triple, Double, Double, Double (T2D3)

While the OECD categories provide a general framework for understanding growth rates, Silicon Valley often operates at a different pace. In his book *Blitzscaling*, Reid Hoffman introduces the T2D3 framework, a rule of thumb for hypergrowth that has become a mantra in the tech world. It stands for **Triple, Triple, Double, Double,**

Double, representing a specific pattern of revenue growth over five consecutive periods (typically quarters or years):

- **Year 1:** Triple revenue
- **Year 2:** Triple revenue again
- **Year 3:** Double revenue
- **Year 4:** Double revenue again
- **Year 5:** Double revenue once more

This aggressive growth trajectory reflects the "blitzscaling" mindset, where companies prioritize speed and market dominance above all else. It's a high-risk, high-reward approach often fueled by venture capital and a winner-takes-all mentality.

Starting with an ARR (Annual Recurring Revenue) of $1M, in Year 1, you triple that to reach $3M ARR. Building on that momentum, in Year 2, you triple the $3M to reach $9M ARR. Now, the pace shifts slightly. In Year 3, you double the $9M to reach $18M ARR. Maintaining this impressive growth, you double the $18M in Year 4 to reach $36M ARR. Finally, in Year 5, you double the $36M to achieve a remarkable $72M ARR. This growth trajectory demonstrates the power of the T2D3 rule, showcasing how a company can achieve exponential growth in a relatively short period.

While pinpointing companies that have *perfectly* followed the T2D3 trajectory is difficult, here are some notable examples of SaaS (Software as a Service) companies that have experienced hypergrowth and achieved substantial scale, embodying the spirit of the T2D3 rule:

- **Salesforce:** a pioneer in cloud-based CRM (Customer Relationship Management), Salesforce experienced phenomenal growth in its early years, rapidly expanding its customer base and revenue. While not a perfect T2D3 fit, its aggressive growth trajectory and market dominance exemplify the blitzscaling mindset.

- **NetSuite:** another early SaaS success story, NetSuite provided cloud-based ERP (Enterprise Resource Planning) solutions for businesses. It experienced rapid growth, expanding its product offerings and customer base significantly, reflecting the ambitious scaling emphasized in the T2D3 rule.

- **Workday:** this provider of enterprise cloud applications for finance and human resources demonstrated impressive growth, capturing a significant market share and achieving a multi-billion dollar valuation. Its rapid expansion aligns with the ambitious targets set by the T2D3 framework.

Zendesk

- **Zendesk:** known for its customer service and engagement platform, Zendesk experienced rapid growth in its early years, expanding its user base and product offerings significantly. Its focus on speed and market share capture reflects the core principles of blitzscaling.

It's crucial to remember that the T2D3 rule is a guideline, not a rigid formula. These companies, while demonstrating impressive growth, may not have precisely followed the T2D3 trajectory. However, their rapid scaling, market dominance, and focus on speed exemplify the blitzscaling mindset that the T2D3 rule represents.

Key takeaways from the T2D3 rule

- **Ambitious growth:** the T2D3 rule sets a tremendously ambitious growth target, pushing companies to expand rapidly and capture market share quickly.
- **Sustained momentum:** it's not just about explosive growth in a single period; it's also about maintaining that momentum over multiple periods, demonstrating a sustainable growth trajectory.
- **Silicon Valley mindset:** this rule reflects the unique culture and expectations of Silicon Valley, where rapid scaling and disruption are often the keys to success.

Important considerations

- **Not for everyone:** the T2D3 rule is not a universal prescription for growth. It's a specific framework for companies operating in winner-takes-all markets, often characterized by network effects and rapid innovation. It also needs significant funding, often the same amount as the revenue generated.
- **Sustainability:** while such hypergrowth can be exhilarating, it's crucial to balance speed with sustainability. Companies need to ensure they have the infrastructure, resources, and organizational capacity to support such rapid expansion.

- **Beyond revenue:** while the T2D3 rule focuses on revenue growth, it's important to consider other metrics as well—profitability, customer satisfaction, and employee morale—to ensure balanced and sustainable growth.

The T2D3 rule provides a fascinating glimpse into the aggressive growth mindset of Silicon Valley. While it may not be suitable for all businesses, it highlights the importance of setting ambitious goals, pushing boundaries, and seizing opportunities in a rapidly evolving world. And that's inspirational.

The rule of 40

The Rule of 40 is a financial metric used to evaluate the performance of fast-growing companies, particularly in the software and SaaS sectors. This rule helps investors and stakeholders balance growth and profitability in a simple formula. The idea is to provide a quick health check on whether a company is managing its growth effectively. Growth should be guided and shaped, not left to chance.

The Rule of 40 states that a company's combined growth rate and profit margin should be at least 40%. You need the growth rate—typically measured as the year-over-year percentage increase in revenue—and the profit margin—be it the operational margin or EBITDA (see Explanation on p. 55).

To apply the Rule of 40, you add the company's growth rate to its profit margin. For example, if a company is growing at 30% per year and has a profit margin of 10%, the combined score is 40%. Or if a company is growing at 20% per year and has a profit margin of 25%, the combined score is 45%.

A combined score of 40% or higher is generally considered good, indicating that the company is in a healthy balance of growth and profitability. Scores below 40% suggest that a company might not be growing fast enough or is not sufficiently profitable, given its growth rate.

The Rule of 40 is particularly useful for evaluating high-growth companies that might not yet be profitable or that are investing heavily in growth at the expense of short-term profitability. It provides a benchmark to ensure that while a company is growing quickly, it isn't burning through cash at an unsustainable rate, or conversely, that it isn't sacrificing growth opportunities to maintain profitability.

Adobe has transitioned successfully from a traditional licensing model to a cloud-based subscription model, which has driven both substantial growth and high profit margins. Adobe often surpasses the Rule of 40 threshold, reflecting its effective management and strong market position.

The Rule of 40 simplifies the complex trade-offs between growth and profitability into a single metric. In other words, short- and long-term. This rule is a simplified assessment tool that doesn't capture all nuances (like market conditions, business model specifics, and the cash flow situation) but offers a quick snapshot of a company's financial health, growth potential, and operational efficiency, useful for investors and founders making comparative assessments across similar companies.

One important remark: companies often think that growth is sacrificial. In other words, you have to endure long periods of low profit to generate growth. That is not always true. **The order is not growth followed by profit,but rather high returns followed by growth.**

Explanation

EBITDA: EBITDA stands for Earnings Before Interest, Taxes, Depreciation, and Amortization. It's a way to measure a company's financial performance without having to factor in accounting, financial, and tax treatments. Think of EBITDA as a way to evaluate a company's performance based on the cash profits it makes from its day-to-day operations, ignoring some of the external factors and accounting decisions that don't directly affect its operating cash flow. It helps to understand how well the company's core business is doing at generating cash, which is useful for comparing companies within the same industry.

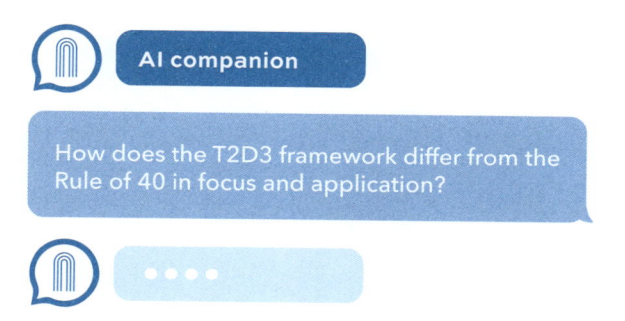

AI companion

How does the T2D3 framework differ from the Rule of 40 in focus and application?

CHAPTER

5

SCALING YOUR BUSINESS

You're going to make mistakes. Relax.

This chapter explores the nuances of growing and scaling, providing insights and strategies to help you navigate your expansion journey effectively. By understanding the difference between these two fundamental concepts, you can make informed decisions that drive sustainable growth and maximize your business's potential.

Growth vs. scaling

While the terms "growth" and "scaling" are often used interchangeably, there is a subtle yet crucial distinction between them. Understanding this difference can significantly impact your strategic choices and your ability to achieve sustainable expansion.

Imagine a farmer planting more seeds to increase their harvest. They're adding more resources—land, labor, seeds—to produce more output. This is analogous to **growing** a business. It typically involves adding more resources—capital, land, employees, or equipment—to increase production and revenue. Revenue generally increases in proportion to the resources invested. The primary goal is to get bigger, expanding the company as a whole.

Now imagine a baker using the same oven to bake more bread by optimizing their baking process. They're increasing output without significantly increasing resources. This is akin to **scaling** a business. It involves generating significantly more revenue with a relatively small increase in resources. Revenue increases at a faster rate than resources invested, leading to improved efficiency and profitability. The primary goal is to become more efficient, optimizing processes and leveraging technology to handle increased volume without a proportional increase in costs.

Feature	Growing	Scaling
Input	Increased	Relatively stable
Output	Increased proportionally	Increased exponentially
Focus	Expansion	Efficiency
Progression	Linear	Exponential
Cost	Higher	Lower
Profitability	Can be lower initially	Higher in the long run

Figure 5 • Growth vs. scaling

Understanding the difference between growth and scaling is crucial. While growth refers to increasing revenue and market share, scaling is about increasing revenue at a much faster rate than costs. Basically, a business is scalable when expenses grow linearly and revenue increases exponentially. In other words, **a scalable business model is one where the addition of new resources brings increasing returns. In simple terms, all scaling involves growth, but not all growth is scaling**. There is no systematic link between sales and profitability. Scaling requires efficient processes, robust systems, and a scalable business model that can handle increased demand without a proportional increase in costs. And there is also one more key ingredient, a real superpower that we will come back to in a moment.

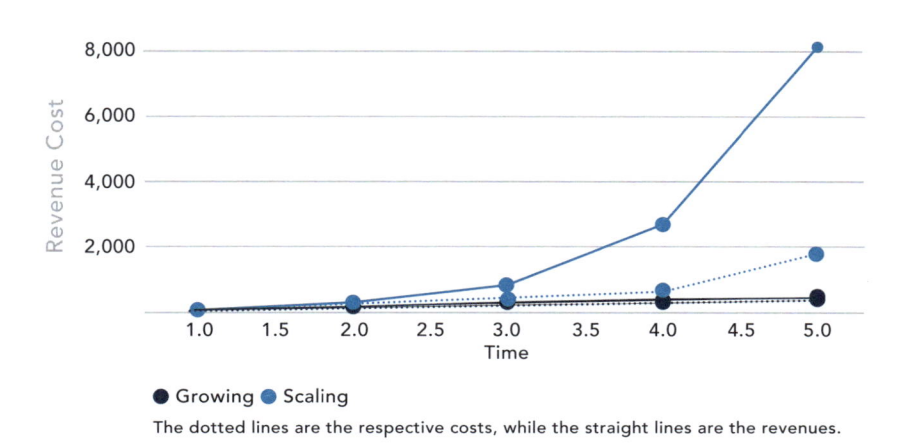

● Growing ● Scaling

The dotted lines are the respective costs, while the straight lines are the revenues.

Figure 6 • Growth vs. scaling: revenue and cost over time

Scaling allows businesses to achieve sustainable growth by maximizing resource utilization and improving profitability. It's about working smarter, not just harder. By optimizing processes, leveraging technology, and building scalable systems, companies can handle increased demand without being constrained by linear resource limitations.

Growing and scaling are not mutually exclusive; they are complementary processes. Companies often go through phases of growing and scaling, adapting their strategies as they evolve. The key is to understand the distinction and choose the right approach for your current stage of development.

Scaling a business is a complex endeavor indeed, involving a multitude of interconnected elements and challenges. It's not a single activity with a straightforward solution, but rather a dynamic system with multiple moving parts that require careful orchestration. However, scaling a business is not typically a "wicked problem"—a problem that is so complex and multifaceted that it defies any definitive solution. It's how you deal with scaling over the course of time that defines your success as a business leader. By understanding the complexities of scaling and implementing effective strategies, businesses can overcome challenges, achieve sustainable growth, and reach their full potential.

The scalability superpower: leveraging intangible assets

In the quest for scalable growth, one often overlooked superpower lies in intangible assets. Unlike physical assets, which are tangible and limited in their capacity, intangible assets possess inherent scalability, allowing businesses to expand their reach and impact without a proportional increase in resources. Let's explore the superpower of intangible assets, highlighting how they can fuel scalable growth and create sustainable competitive advantage.

Intangible assets are non-physical resources that have value and contribute to a company's profitability. They are often knowledge-based, innovative, or creative in nature, and their value lies in their potential to generate future revenue and growth. Some key categories of intangible assets include intellectual property, brand equity, data, proprietary or third-party software, and technology in general.

Intangible assets possess inherent scalability due to their non-physical nature. They can be replicated, distributed, and leveraged across multiple channels and markets without significant additional costs. This allows businesses to reach a wider audience, personalize experiences, automate processes, and best of all, build network effects.

Think about applications where a strong brand can be leveraged through franchising, allowing businesses to expand rapidly by licensing their brand and operating model to franchisees. Or companies like Netflix and Amazon that use data to personalize recommendations and offers, driving customer engagement and sales. Obviously, also SaaS companies like Salesforce and Adobe that provide cloud-based software solutions where new customers and users add near-zero costs but generate attractive recurring revenue that enables scalable growth.

The same goes for music streaming where platforms like Spotify and Apple Music leverage digital music libraries to provide on-demand access to millions of songs, reaching a global audience with minimal marginal costs.

Leveraging digital technology is how Snapchat reached 200 million users with just a team of 300 people. Or, even more impressive, how Instagram reached 300 million users with a team of only 13.

Developing and protecting intangible assets is crucial for achieving scalable growth, including investing in innovation, protecting intellectual property, building a strong brand, and monetizing data. Bits rather than atoms are the true DNA of scalability.

By strategically building and leveraging intangible assets, businesses can unlock a powerful engine for scalable growth, creating a sustainable competitive advantage and achieving lasting success in the marketplace.

Architecting scalability: attributes of a scalable business model

Scalability isn't merely an outcome; it's a design principle. It's about building a business model that inherently supports rapid expansion without a proportional increase in resources. Let's delve into the key attributes and characteristics of scalable business models, exploring how companies can architect their operations, offerings, and strategies to achieve sustainable growth.

At the heart of scalable business models lie intangible assets. These non-physical resources allow businesses to expand their reach and impact without being constrained by physical limitations. By leveraging intangible assets, companies can create offerings that are easily replicated, distributed, and personalized, fueling efficient growth.

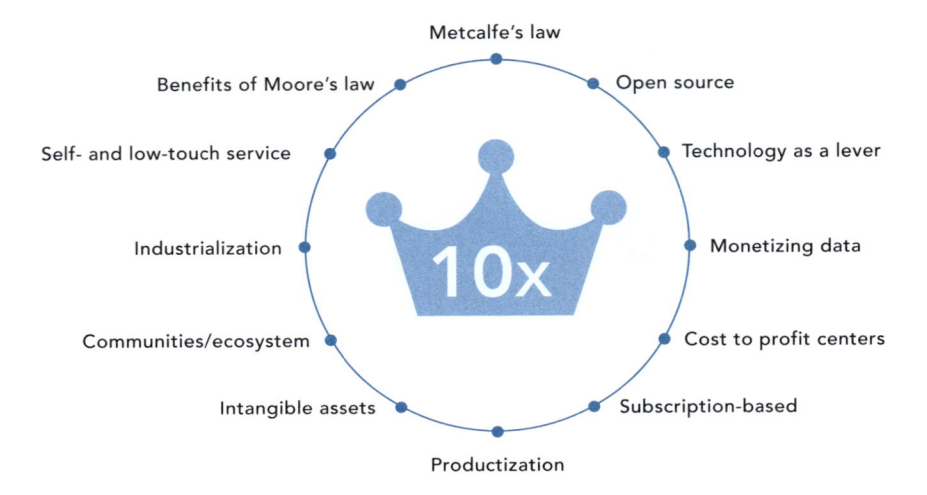

Figure 7 • Key attributes of scalable business models

Leveraging network effects

Network effects, also called Metcalfe's law, occur when the value of a product or service increases with each new user. Platforms like Meta, Airbnb, and Uber thrive on network effects, creating a powerful growth engine where users attract more users, leading to exponential growth.

Embracing open source

Open-source software and technologies can accelerate scalability by providing access to a vast pool of collaborative development and innovation. By leveraging open-source tools, companies can reduce development costs, increase flexibility, and tap into a global community of contributors. Odoo, Elastic, MariaDB, Aleph Alpha, Mistral, and Guardsquare have embraced that model with great success.

Harnessing technology as a lever

Technology, particularly digital technology, is a key enabler of scalability. Automation, cloud computing, and data analytics allow businesses to streamline operations, personalize experiences, and reach a global audience with minimal marginal costs.

Subscription-based models

Subscription models provide recurring revenue streams, creating predictability and stability that support scalable growth. By offering subscription-based access to their products or services, companies can foster customer loyalty and generate consistent cash flow. It's the most popular model for unicorns, such as UiPath, Intercom, Pipedrive, and Collibra.

Productization of services

Transforming services into standardized products enables scalability by creating repeatable processes and reducing reliance on individual expertise. This allows businesses to deliver consistent quality and expand their service offerings efficiently.

Industrialization

Applying industrial principles like standardization, modularization, and process optimization can significantly enhance scalability. By streamlining operations and creating repeatable processes, companies can increase efficiency and handle increased volume without a proportional increase in costs.

Self- and low-touch services

Empowering customers to serve themselves through online platforms, automated tools, and comprehensive resources can significantly reduce the need for human intervention, enabling scalable growth without a corresponding increase in customer support costs.

Moore's law and exponential technologies

Moore's law, which predicts the doubling of computing power every two years, has profound implications for scalability. Think of it like this: the people you will hire in 18 months will be twice as smart and half as expensive as the ones you hire today. As technology advances exponentially, businesses can leverage increasingly powerful and affordable tools.

Monetizing and valorizing data

Data is a valuable asset that can be monetized and leveraged for scalable growth. By collecting, analyzing, and utilizing data, companies can personalize experiences, optimize operations, and create new revenue streams. Springworks, NxtPort, Hoplr, and Tink all have a data monetization business model.

Creating a community/ecosystem

Building a strong community or ecosystem around your product or service can foster engagement, loyalty, and organic growth. By creating a platform for users to connect, share, and collaborate, companies can tap into the power of collective intelligence and accelerate their growth trajectory. For inspiration, look at SoundCloud, Tattoodo, DriveTribe, Fishbrain, and Opportunity Network.

Scalability is not just about growing bigger; it's about growing smarter. By embracing these attributes and designing their business models for scalability, companies can achieve rapid expansion, maximize resource utilization, and create a sustainable competitive advantage in the marketplace.

Business model vs. operating model

While designing a scalable business model is crucial, it's equally important to consider the scalability of your operating model. The operating model encompasses the people, processes, and technology that enable the execution of your business model. It's the engine that drives your operations and delivers value to your customers.

It's often easier to design a scalable business model than to create a scalable operating model. A business model can leverage technology, network effects, and intangible assets to achieve scalability, but the operating model requires aligning people, processes, and culture, which can be more challenging.

However, a scalable operating model is essential for sustained growth. It's about creating an organization that can efficiently handle increased volume, adapt to change, and maintain quality and consistency as it expands.

Typical elements of scalability in an operating model are:
Automation: automating repetitive tasks and processes can significantly enhance efficiency and reduce reliance on manual labor, enabling scalability without a proportional increase in headcount.

Data accessibility: empowering employees with access to data and analytics can improve decision-making, foster a data-driven culture, and enable more agile responses to market changes.

Process optimization: streamlining workflows, eliminating bottlenecks, and continuously improving processes can enhance efficiency and scalability.

Technology adoption: embracing new technologies and platforms can enable data analysis and remote collaboration, supporting scalable growth.

Culture of empowerment: fostering a culture of empowerment, where employees are encouraged to take ownership and make decisions, can enhance agility and responsiveness, crucial for scaling effectively.

By focusing on these elements, companies can create operating models that support scalable growth, ensuring that their internal capabilities can keep pace with their ambitions.

AI companion

What is the fundamental difference between 'grow' and 'scale' in a business context?

 ● ● ● ●

What elements are essential to make an operational model scalable, and why are they important?

 ● ● ● ●

In what situations would focusing on scalability not be an effective strategy?

 ● ● ● ●

How can companies ensure that their scalability remains sustainable and not at the expense of quality or customer satisfaction?

 ● ● ● ●

STRATEGIC APPROACHES TO GROWTH

The perfect size for an organization is BIG enough to COPE, SMALL enough to CARE.

Simplifying strategic choices: the three components of a business

To navigate the complexities of growth and scaling, it's helpful to simplify our understanding of what constitutes a business. At its core, any business can be broken down into three fundamental components:

1. **Offering:** this is what the business provides to its customers, whether it's a tangible product or an intangible service. It encompasses the features, benefits, and value proposition that address customer needs and differentiate the business in the marketplace.

2. **Go-to-market:** this represents the channels and strategies used to reach and engage the target market. It includes marketing,

sales, distribution, and customer service, encompassing all the activities involved in delivering the offering to the customer.

3. **Market segment:** this defines the specific group of customers the business aims to serve. It involves segmenting the market based on factors like demographics, needs, behaviors, and preferences, allowing the business to tailor its offering and go-to-market approach effectively.

The go-to-market bridge

Figure 8 • Go-to-market bridge

The go-to-market strategy acts as a bridge, connecting the offering with the chosen market segment. It's the critical link that determines how effectively a business can reach its target customers, deliver its value proposition, and ultimately achieve its growth objectives.

A business can choose to build its own go-to-market bridge, it can decide to ally with partners, or it can buy parties that have a bridge in place. Of course, it can decide to combine all three, as long as it is careful not to create a so-called channel conflict. A channel conflict arises when there is a clash or incompatibility between different distribution channels used by a business to reach its customers. This can occur when a company sells its products or services through multiple channels. Channel conflicts can manifest in various ways, including pricing discrepancies, brand inconsistency, and competition between channels.

Build: the direct approach

Figure 9 • Build

One fundamental strategic choice a company can make is to go direct, building its own channels to reach its target market. This could involve establishing a physical store, creating an e-commerce website, building an (internal) sales team, or developing a direct marketing strategy.

Going direct offers businesses greater control over the customer experience, branding, and messaging, allowing you to cultivate stronger customer relationships and potentially achieve higher profit margins by eliminating intermediaries. This direct interaction also generates valuable data and insights into customer preferences and behaviors. It enables continuous testing of different marketing messages, sales strategies, and customer service approaches to optimize your direct channels.

However, this approach requires significant upfront investment in infrastructure, technology, and personnel, potentially leading to slower market reach and greater complexity in managing these channels. Additionally, going direct carries higher risk, as the success of these channels depends entirely on the company's ability to execute effectively. In practice, slower growth and higher initial investment are the biggest challenges.

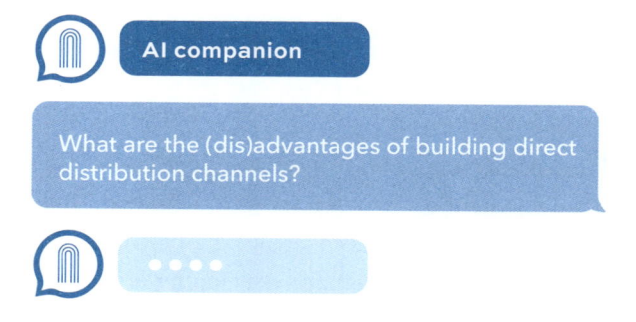

AI companion

What are the (dis)advantages of building direct distribution channels?

Ally: the indirect approach

In the dynamic landscape of business, growth often hinges on strategic collaboration. This section explores the power of alliances and partnerships, highlighting how companies can leverage collaborative relationships to accelerate their growth trajectory, expand their reach, and achieve shared success.

An alliance or partnership is a collaborative agreement between two or more independent companies to achieve common goals, share resources, and create mutual benefits. These relationships can take various forms, from joint ventures and strategic alliances to licensing agreements, partnerships (collaborating with other businesses to leverage their existing channels and customer base), resellers (selling through intermediaries like retailers or distributors), online marketplaces (leveraging platforms like Amazon or Bol.com to reach a wider audience), and affiliate marketing (partnering with third parties to promote the offering in exchange for a commission).

Figure 10 • Ally

Partnerships often start with high expectations that do not crystalize in the expected timeframe. Frie Pétré, founder of Qollabi, compares this to the Gartner hype cycle.

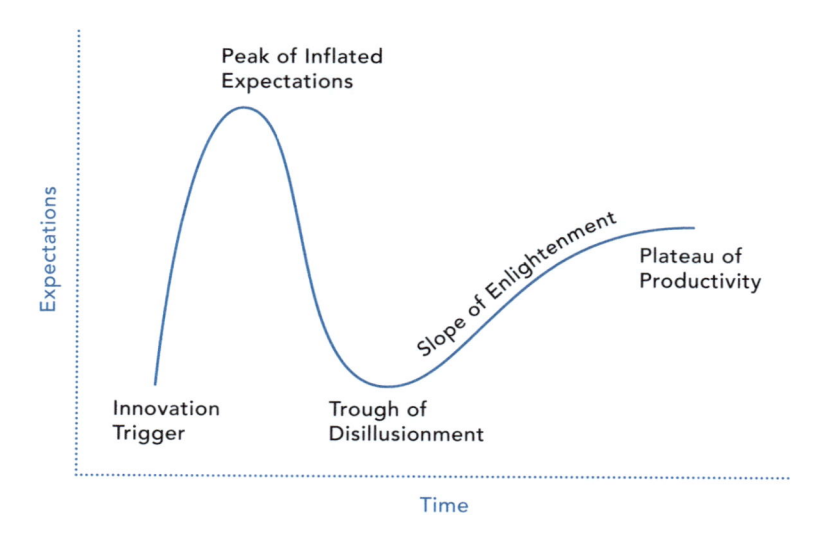

Figure 11 • Partner hype cycle

However, even when you consider working with partners, always start direct to gather firsthand experience: begin by establishing direct channels to interact directly with your customers, gather firsthand experience about their needs and preferences, and refine your offering and go-to-market approach. This foundation of knowledge and customer understanding can then inform your strategy for expanding into indirect channels later on.

Buy: acquisition(s)

Buying through acquisitions offers an alternative pathway to expansion, allowing companies to accelerate their growth trajectory by acquiring existing businesses. An acquisition occurs when one company purchases a majority stake or all of another company's assets, gaining control over its operations, resources, and customer base.

Acquisitions can be a powerful tool for growth, enabling companies to expand market share, acquire new capabilities, enter new markets, gain access to talent, or achieve synergies. But they also carry significant risks and challenges. By carefully considering strategic fit, conducting thorough due diligence, and planning for effective integration, companies can increase their chances of successful acquisitions and leverage this pathway to achieve their growth objectives.

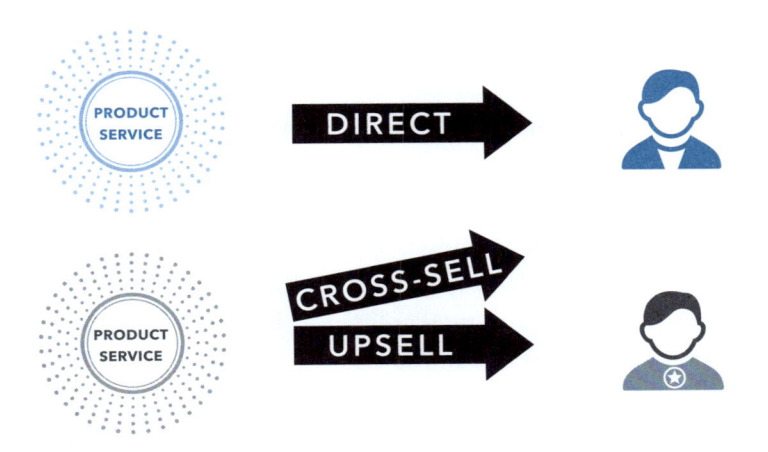

Figure 12 • Buy

Different types of acquisitions

- **Horizontal acquisition:** acquiring a company in the same industry and stage of the value chain, often a competitor.
- **Vertical acquisition:** acquiring a company at a different stage of the value chain, such as a supplier or distributor.
- **Conglomerate acquisition:** acquiring a company in an unrelated industry, diversifying the business portfolio.
- **Concentric acquisition:** acquiring a company in a related industry or with complementary products or services.

The rationale behind an acquisition can vary significantly depending on the acquiring company's strategic goals and the specific assets and characteristics of the target company. While sometimes it's a combination of factors, often one primary reason drives the acquisition. It can be about the offering to enhance or replace a product, a technology, or intellectual property. Or the channels to expand market reach, often in a specific geography or segment, and strengthen distribution and online presence. Lastly, the rationale is to access the customer base of the acquisition target. All this allows for next, upselling, and cross-selling.

While one primary reason often drives an acquisition, it's common for a combination of factors to influence the decision. For example, a company might acquire another for its technology and its customer base, or for its product line and its distribution channels.

Understanding the primary rationale behind an acquisition is crucial for effective integration and achieving the desired strategic outcomes. By clearly identifying the key assets and capabilities being acquired, companies can develop a focused integration plan and maximize the value of the acquisition. This process is called Post-Merger Integration (PMI). PMI is the process of combining two or more companies into a single, unified entity after an acquisition. It involves integrating various aspects of the businesses, including operations, technology, culture, and human resources. Effective PMI is essential for realizing the intended benefits of the acquisition and minimizing potential risks and disruptions. Successful PMI requires careful planning, effective leadership, and a focus on communication, collaboration, and cultural integration. By addressing these key aspects, companies can increase their chances of realizing the intended benefits of the acquisition and achieving their strategic growth objectives.

Build, buy or ally?

The matrix on p. 80 provides a valuable tool for strategic decision-making, helping businesses weigh the pros and cons of different growth approaches and choose the most suitable option based on their specific circumstances, urgency, and risk tolerance.

	BUILD	BUY	ALLY
HIGH URGENCY	Slow	Fast	Fast
HIGH UNCERTAINTY	Failure likely unsaleable	Failure potentially unsaleable	Share losses and retain buy option
SOFT CAPABILITIES IMPORTANT	Cultural consistency	Culture and valuation problems	Culture and control problems
HIGHLY MODULAR CAPABILITIES	Develop in new venture unit	Problem of buying whole company	Ally just with relevant partner unit

Source: SlideGeeks 1

Figure 13 • Build, buy or ally?

In short: building is slow but offers control, suitable for modular capabilities and when urgency is low. Buying is faster but riskier, ideal when urgency is high and cultural fit is strong. Allying offers a balance, sharing risks and providing flexibility, but requires careful partner selection and management.

Get, keep, and grow: maximizing customer value for growth

While acquiring new customers is essential for any business, sustainable growth hinges on more than just customer acquisition. It requires a holistic approach that encompasses not only getting new customers but also keeping existing ones and encouraging them to grow their relationship with your business.

$$\Big(\text{UP \& CROSS-SELL} \Big) \Big(\text{USAGE} \Big) \Big(\text{RETENTION} \Big)$$

Figure 14 • Get, keep, and grow

In the traditional business landscape, it's not uncommon to find a disproportionate focus on customer acquisition. Many businesses dedicate the majority of their resources and efforts to acquiring new customers, often neglecting the potential that lies within their existing customer base.

A typical business might allocate its resources as follows:
- Acquisitions: 90%
- Retention: 8% (with the positive exception of subscription businesses)
- Growing existing customers: 2%

This imbalance reflects a common mindset that prioritizes new customer acquisition above all else. However, this approach often overlooks the significant opportunities for growth and profitability that can be achieved by focusing on existing customers.

A more balanced approach would be to shift the allocation of resources toward a more holistic customer lifecycle strategy, such as:

- Acquisitions: 50%
- Retention: 30%
- Growing existing customers: 20%

This revised allocation ensures that while customer acquisition remains important, equal importance is given to retaining existing customers and nurturing their growth. This balanced approach recognizes that existing customers are a valuable asset that can contribute significantly to a business's long-term success.

By dedicating more time and resources to understanding the needs of existing customers, businesses can identify opportunities to help them grow and expand their relationship with the company. This could involve providing personalized solutions, offering upselling or cross-selling opportunities, or simply staying in touch and providing ongoing support.

The frequency with which businesses should focus on helping their customers grow depends on various factors, such as the nature of the business, the customer lifecycle, and the overall growth strategy. However, it's essential to make this a regular and ongoing part of the business's customer relationship management approach.

By actively seeking ways to help customers grow, businesses not only strengthen customer relationships and foster loyalty but also create a powerful engine for their own growth and success.

Retention trumps growth

In Aesop's fable of the tortoise and the hare, the speedy hare, confident in its quickness, takes a nap during the race, allowing the slow and steady tortoise to ultimately win. This classic tale offers a valuable lesson for businesses focused on growth: while rapid acquisition might seem like the fastest path to success, sustainable growth often hinges on the tortoise-like persistence of customer retention.

Retention, like the tortoise, steadily adds and keeps value within the company. It's the compounding effect of loyal customers returning for repeat business, generating recurring revenue, and contributing to long-term profitability. In that sense, retention is akin to the most powerful force in the universe: **compound interest**.

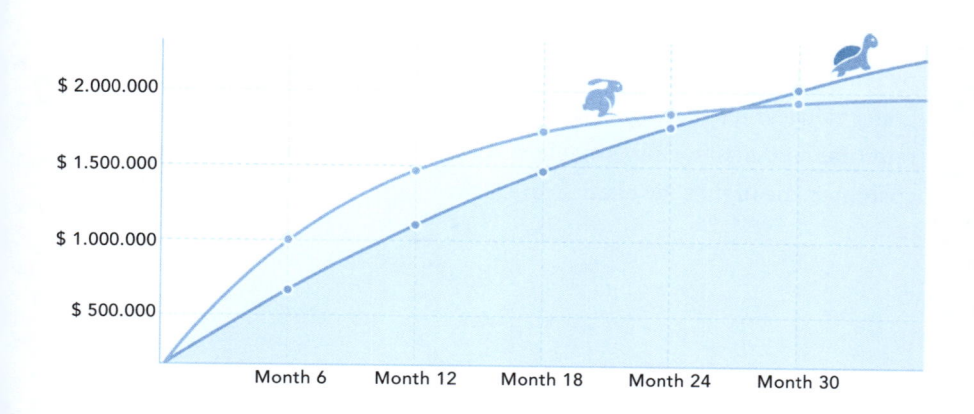

Figure 15 • Retention trumps growth

The graph above illustrates this principle. It simulates two SaaS businesses:

- **The hare:** this company boasts high acquisition performance, rapidly gaining new customers. However, it also suffers from higher churn, losing customers at a faster rate.
- **The tortoise:** this company has a slower acquisition rate but excels at retention, keeping its customers for longer periods.

As the simulation demonstrates, the tortoise eventually overtakes the hare. While the hare enjoys an initial burst of growth, its high churn rate eventually catches up, limiting its long-term revenue potential. The tortoise, on the other hand, steadily builds its customer base, and its lower churn rate allows it to accumulate and retain more value over time.

This visualization underscores the importance of balancing acquisition with retention. While acquiring new customers is essential, neglecting retention can undermine long-term growth and profitability. By focusing on building strong customer relationships, providing ongoing value, and fostering loyalty, businesses can unlock the power of retention and achieve sustainable success. Note that the smaller the customer, the higher the chance for churn.

The unicorn combination: high acquisition and high retention

While the tortoise-and-hare analogy highlights the importance of balancing acquisition and retention, the true magic happens when a company manages to excel at both. This is the "unicorn" scenario, where the business not only attracts new customers at a rapid pace but also keeps them engaged and loyal over the long term.

Imagine a company that combines the hare's speed with the tortoise's endurance. This company would not only capture a significant market share quickly but also build a loyal customer base that generates recurring revenue and fuels sustainable growth. This combination is often the key to achieving "unicorn" status, a term used to describe privately held startup companies valued at over $1 billion.

Achieving this magical combination requires a multifaceted approach such as a strong value proposition, effective marketing and sales, exceptional customer experience, continuous innovation, or building a thriving community.

By mastering both acquisition and retention, companies can unlock exponential growth potential, building a sustainable and highly valuable business that stands out in the competitive landscape.

Beyond service: the art of customer retention

While acquiring new customers is essential for growth, true success lies in building lasting relationships with your existing customer base. Many businesses assume that providing good service or a quality product will automatically lead to customer retention. While these are undoubtedly crucial foundations, retention requires a more holistic approach that nurtures the customer relationship beyond the initial transaction.

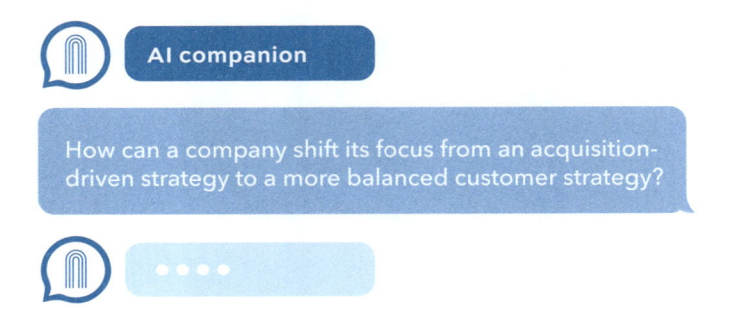

AI companion

How can a company shift its focus from an acquisition-driven strategy to a more balanced customer strategy?

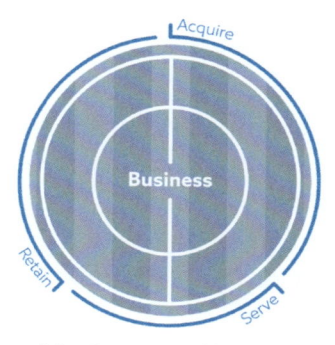

Figure 16 • Business is like a sports game

Serving focuses on meeting immediate customer needs and expectations during their interaction with your business. It involves providing excellent customer service, delivering quality products, and resolving issues effectively.

Retaining goes beyond serving. It's about building a long-term relationship with the customer, fostering loyalty, and encouraging repeat business. It involves staying engaged with customers, understanding their evolving needs, and continuously providing value to keep them coming back for more.

While serving customers well is essential, retention requires a deeper commitment to building relationships, understanding needs, and providing ongoing value. By mastering the art of customer retention, businesses can create a sustainable-growth engine that drives profitability, loyalty, and long-term success. Another way of looking at it is that **acquisition represents the level of excitement for an offering, whereas retention describes the love that your customers feel for who you are.**

Optimize and capture more value

While the pursuit of growth often focuses on acquiring new customers, as we saw in the previous section, there is a parallel path to expansion that lies within your existing offerings. Let's explore the power of optimizing and maximizing the value you extract from your current products or services. By strategically focusing on cost reduction, cash flow enhancement, and pricing optimization, businesses can unlock significant growth potential without solely relying on new customer acquisition.

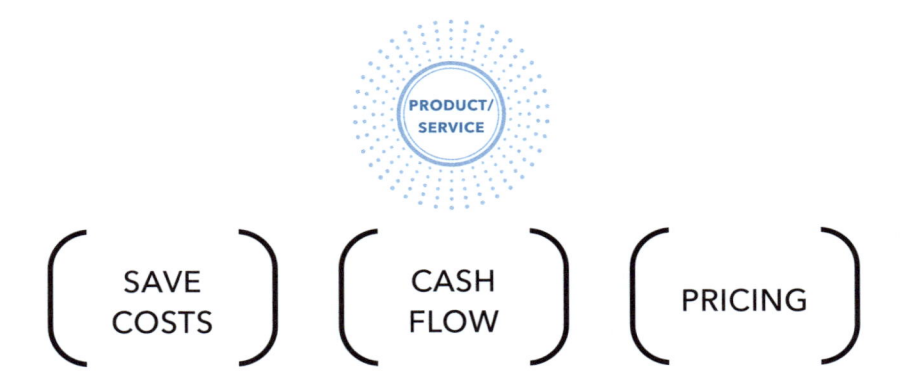

Figure 17 • Optimize and capture more value

The central placement of "Product/Service" in this visual emphasizes that these three levers are ultimately focused on optimizing the value derived from the core offering. Whether it's through cost reduction, cash flow improvement, or pricing optimization, the goal is to maximize the profitability and sustainability of the product or service.

Let's look at the three core levers that businesses can pull to drive growth and profitability.

1. Save costs

This lever focuses on increasing efficiency and reducing operational costs. By streamlining processes, negotiating better deals with suppliers, leveraging technology, and optimizing resource allocation, businesses can free up capital to reinvest in growth initiatives or improve their bottom line.

2. Cash flow

Healthy cash flow is the lifeblood of any growing business. This lever emphasizes strategies to improve cash flow management, such as optimizing payment terms, reducing inventory holding costs, and accelerating collections. Strong cash flow provides the financial flexibility to invest in growth opportunities, weather economic downturns, and maintain a healthy financial position.

3. Pricing

Pricing strategies play a crucial role in capturing value and driving growth. This lever involves analyzing customer perception of value, competitor pricing, and cost structures to optimize pricing models. This could involve implementing value-based pricing, tiered pricing, or dynamic pricing strategies to maximize revenue and profitability.

By effectively managing these three levers, businesses can increase profitability, free up capital for growth, enhance competitiveness, and improve customer satisfaction.

CHAPTER

7

EXTERNAL VS. INTERNAL GROWTH

"All brands are smaller than they want to be." **Byron Sharp**

Balancing the scales

While much of the discussion on growth focuses on external strategies like market penetration and customer acquisition, sustainable expansion requires a harmonious balance between external and internal development. This chapter explores the crucial interplay between external growth (go-to-market) and internal growth (organizational maturity), highlighting the importance of aligning these two forces to achieve lasting success.

The following graph illustrates the relationship between external and internal growth.

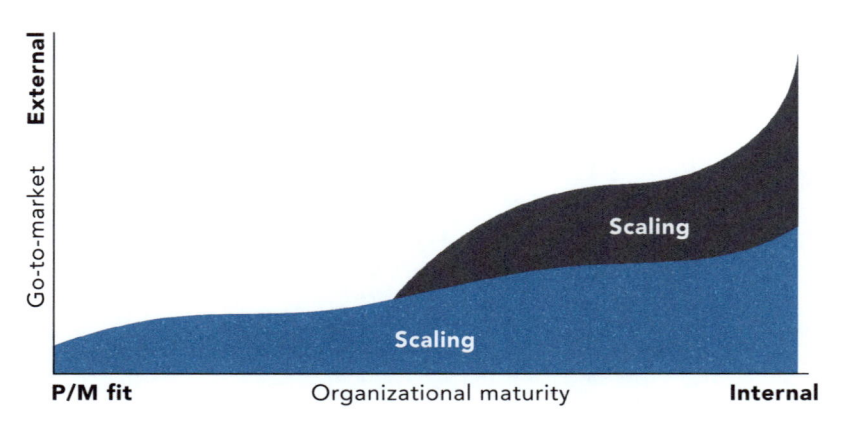

Figure 18 • The relationship between external and internal growth

External growth (go-to-market): this dimension encompasses all the activities involved in reaching and engaging your target market, including marketing and sales. It's about expanding your reach, acquiring new customers, and increasing your market share.

Internal growth (organizational maturity): this dimension focuses on developing the internal capabilities and infrastructure needed to support external growth. It involves strengthening your organization, implementing customer service, optimizing your processes, and fostering a culture that can handle increased complexity and scale.

Sustainable growth requires these two dimensions to be in equilibrium. Focusing solely on external growth, without the internal capacity to support it, is like building a house of cards—it might rise quickly, but it's inherently unstable and prone to collapse. Conversely, building a robust organization without external growth to fuel it is like someone passing away in full health—all the internal systems are functioning perfectly, but there is no life force driving it forward.

The two lines on the graph represent different scaling trajectories. The steeper line signifies a more rapid pace of external growth, which puts greater stress on the organization. While some pressure is healthy and can drive innovation and efficiency, excessive stress can lead to breakdowns in processes, people, and infrastructure. Companies need to carefully manage their growth rate to ensure their internal capabilities can keep pace with their external ambitions, and vice versa.

Premature scaling

When startups raise capital, there is often pressure to scale quickly and demonstrate rapid growth to investors. However, if this external growth isn't supported by a solid foundation of internal capabilities and a validated business model, it can lead to a mismatch between the company's ambitions and its ability to execute.

Investing in internal growth without corresponding external growth can lead to a situation where the company has built up significant infrastructure and resources but lacks the market demand or revenue to sustain them. This can result in a financial crunch, forcing the company to downsize, pivot, or even shut down.

On the other hand, prioritizing external growth without investing in internal capabilities can lead to operational inefficiencies, customer service issues, and an inability to fulfill promises made during the acquisition phase. This can damage the company's reputation, increase churn, and ultimately hinder its growth prospects.

By taking a measured and strategic approach to scaling, startups can increase their chances of success and avoid the dead-end street of premature expansion.

External growth

External growth hinges on effectively reaching and engaging your target market. This involves choosing the right channels to connect with potential customers, deliver your value proposition, and build a thriving business. Remember, if you get customers, you have power.

The image to the right offers a glimpse into the vast array of external growth channels available to businesses today. From traditional approaches like M&A (Mergers and Acquisitions) and branch expansion to digital strategies like SEO (Search Engine Optimization), content marketing, and social media, the options are plentiful and ever-evolving. This diverse landscape presents both opportunities and challenges for businesses seeking to expand their reach and acquire new customers.

Navigating this labyrinth of channels can be daunting. Making the right choices requires a deep understanding of your target market, your business model, and your competitive landscape.

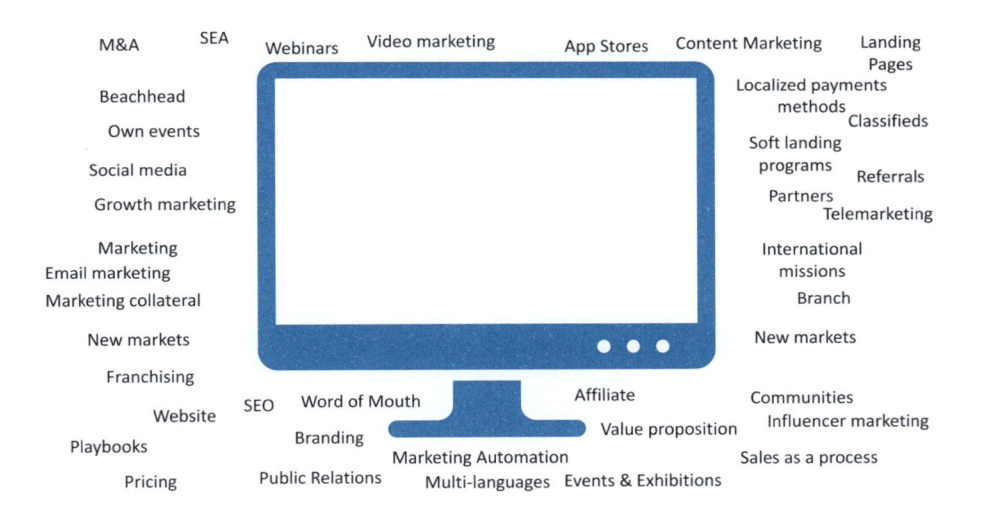

Figure 19 • Landscape of external growth channels

The landscape of external growth channels is constantly evolving. What works today might be obsolete tomorrow. New channels emerge, existing channels evolve, and customer preferences shift at a dizzying pace. This dynamic environment demands agility, adaptability, and a willingness to experiment and innovate.

While traditional channels like bank branches once enjoyed decades of dominance, the digital age has accelerated the rate of change. Digital channels, in particular, can rise and fall with remarkable speed.

Social-media platforms gain and lose popularity, new marketing technologies emerge, and customer behaviors shift rapidly. This requires businesses to stay informed, adapt their strategies, and continuously evaluate the effectiveness of their chosen channels.

To effectively navigate this dynamic landscape, businesses need to understand the customer's journey and preferences to choose channels that align with their needs and behaviors. Continuously track the performance of your channels, analyze data, and adapt your strategy to stay ahead of the curve. And be willing to experiment with new channels and approaches to identify what works best for your business.

Internal growth

While external growth focuses on expanding your reach and acquiring new customers, internal growth is about strengthening your foundation and developing the internal capabilities needed to support sustainable expansion.

The image to the right showcases a diverse range of areas that contribute to internal growth. From essential functions like HR, finance, and legal to strategic areas like product development, data management, and organizational design, internal growth requires a holistic approach that encompasses all aspects of the business.

Just as with external growth channels, navigating the landscape of internal growth requires strategic choices and prioritization. Resources are limited, and businesses need to carefully allocate their investments to maximize impact and support their overall growth strategy.

Internal and external growth are interconnected and mutually reinforcing. Investing in internal capabilities enables businesses to effectively pursue external growth opportunities, while external growth provides the resources and motivation to further strengthen internal foundations.

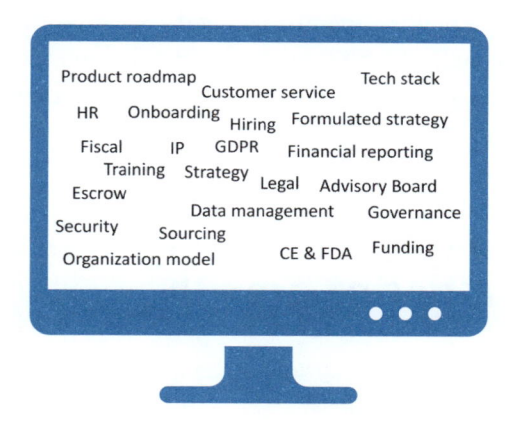

Figure 20 • Landscape of internal growth channels

Organizational maturity refers to the level of development and sophistication of a company's internal systems, processes, and capabilities. A mature organization exhibits characteristics such as well-defined processes and structures, strong leadership and talent, effective communication and collaboration, data-driven decision-making, and adaptability and resilience. A mature organization is better equipped to handle the complexities of growth, scale its operations efficiently, and maintain consistency and quality as it expands.

On the other hand, the operating model encompasses the people, processes, and technology that enable a company to execute its business model. It's the engine that drives daily operations, delivers value to customers, and supports the achievement of business goals. A scalable operating model is essential for sustainable growth. It should be designed to support increased volume, adapt to change, enable innovation, and maximize resource utilization.

By developing a mature organization and a scalable operating model, businesses can create a strong foundation for sustainable growth, ensuring that their internal capabilities can keep pace with their external ambitions.

The strategic lens: navigating the complexities of growth

The image to the right encapsulates the multifaceted nature of running a business. It's the visual representation of the countless decisions, both internal and external, that leaders must grapple with as they navigate the path to sustainable growth. From choosing the right go-to-market channels and building internal capabilities to optimizing customer relationships and fostering a culture of innovation, the possibilities are vast and the challenges are ever-present. As an answer to this complexity, good architecture is simple. Simplicity is the godfather of scaling. Simplicity is the most important design principle for an organization's architecture. Choose the simplest design that gets the job done. The rest will add complexity and friction and, therefore, waste and cost.

This dynamic environment, where markets shift, technologies evolve, and customer preferences change at a rapid pace, adds another layer of complexity. What worked yesterday might not work today, and what works today might be obsolete tomorrow. This constant state of flux can make decision-making feel like navigating a minefield, with potential pitfalls lurking at every turn.

This is where the power of strategy comes into play. Strategy provides a lens through which to view this complex landscape, helping businesses make informed choices, prioritize their efforts, and allocate their resources effectively. It's about understanding the interconnectedness of various factors, anticipating challenges, and seizing opportunities in a constantly evolving environment.

Figure 21 • Navigating the complexities of growth: internal and external growth channels

So far, we have explored various facets of growth and scaling, from strategic frameworks and customer lifecycle management to the importance of intangible assets and organizational maturity. We have examined different pathways to growth, including organic development, acquisitions, and alliances, highlighting the key considerations for each approach.

The journey of growth is a complex and challenging one, but with a clear strategic vision and a commitment to continuous improvement, businesses can navigate the labyrinth, overcome obstacles, and achieve lasting success.

Strategic clustering: simplifying external growth choices

In the face of overwhelming options for external growth, businesses need a way to simplify their decision-making and prioritize their efforts. Clustering involves grouping similar or related items together to create a more organized and manageable structure. In the context of external growth, this means grouping related channels, strategies, and initiatives into clusters based on their shared characteristics, target audience, or strategic goals.

Strategic clustering offers numerous benefits for businesses seeking to optimize their external growth efforts. Simplifying the decision-making process by grouping related options reduces complexity and allows for easier evaluation and comparison of different approaches. This enhanced focus enables businesses to concentrate their resources and efforts on the most impactful areas for growth, ensuring that different initiatives are aligned with overall business goals and strategic priorities. Moreover, clustering can lead to increased efficiency by grouping related activities, maximizing the impact of resources and investments.

Figure 22 • External growth choices

The clustering process involves identifying potential growth options, grouping these options based on shared characteristics, labeling and defining each cluster, and prioritizing clusters based on their potential impact and alignment with business goals.

It's important to recognize that some clusters may influence each other more than others. For example, investments in branding and marketing might significantly impact the effectiveness of sales and distribution channels. Understanding these interdependencies can help businesses make more informed decisions about resource allocation and prioritization.

The external growth landscape is constantly evolving, so your clusters and priorities may need to adapt over time (but less fast than the individual activities). Regularly review and reassess your clusters to ensure they remain relevant and aligned with your business goals and the changing market dynamics.

Your top 3 priorities

Now it's your turn! Based on your business goals, resources, and target market, identify your top 3 priority clusters for external growth:

1. ....

2. ....

3. ....

Strategic clustering: simplifying internal growth choices

While external growth focuses on expanding your market reach and acquiring new customers, internal growth is equally crucial for achieving sustainable success. It involves strengthening your foundation and developing the internal capabilities needed to support your expansion.

Just as with external growth, clustering can be a powerful tool for simplifying decision-making and prioritizing investments in internal capabilities. By grouping related initiatives and functions, businesses can gain a clearer picture of their internal landscape and identify the areas that will contribute most significantly to their growth objectives.

Figure 23 • Internal growth choices

Based on your business goals, resources, and growth strategy, identify your top 3 priority clusters for internal growth:

1. ....

2. ....

3. ....

When reassessing your priorities, it's crucial to recognize that the dynamic nature of the business environment may require adjustments to your strategic direction. This could involve identifying initiatives or activities that are no longer as impactful or aligned with your evolving goals. Be open to the possibility of reducing your investment in certain areas or even stopping them altogether to free up resources and focus on more promising opportunities. This willingness to adapt and re-prioritize is essential for maintaining agility and maximizing your growth potential in a constantly changing market.

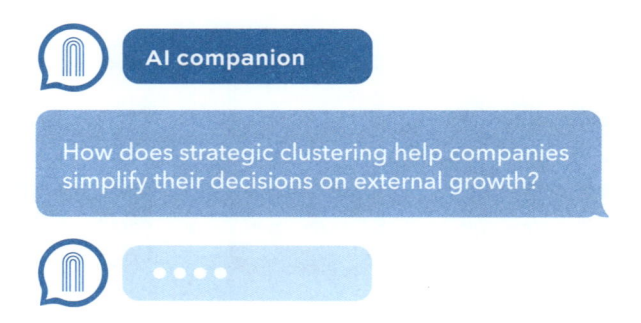

AI companion

How does strategic clustering help companies simplify their decisions on external growth?

The growth profile: scaling yourself to scale your business

Growing a company is not just about expanding operations, acquiring customers, or increasing revenue. It's also about personal growth, about developing the skills, knowledge, and mindset needed to lead and navigate the complexities of a scaling business. Let's dive deeper into the concept of the growth profile, highlighting the key attributes and capabilities that individuals need to cultivate to effectively drive company growth.

The image on p. 106 depicts a portrait divided into two halves, representing the duality of personal and professional growth. It highlights four key elements:

1. **Growth profile:** this refers to the overall set of skills, knowledge, and attributes that enable an individual to contribute to and thrive in a growth environment.
2. **Domain expertise:** this encompasses the deep knowledge and understanding of the industry, market, and business functions relevant to the company's operations.
3. **Experiment design:** this involves the ability to design and carry out experiments, analyze data, and adapt strategies based on results, fostering a culture of innovation and learning.
4. **Tool stack:** this represents the mastery of tools and technologies that enable and support the execution of growth strategies.

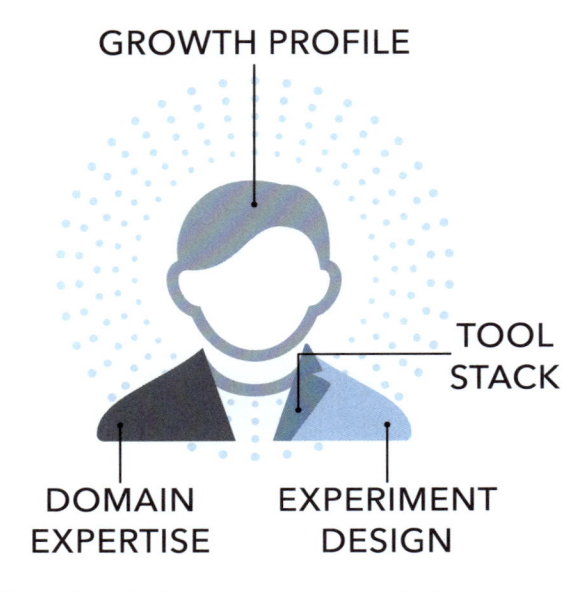

Figure 24 • Duality of personal and professional growth

As a company grows, the demands on its leaders and employees also increase. Personal growth and company growth are intrinsically linked. As individuals develop their skills and knowledge, they become better equipped to contribute to the company's success. Conversely, the challenges and opportunities of a growing company provide a fertile ground for personal development and learning. Growth is a journey. Both personal and professional growth are ongoing journeys that require continuous learning, adaptation, and self-reflection. View challenges as opportunities for growth and development, pushing yourself beyond your comfort zone to expand your capabilities. Invest in yourself and dedicate time and resources to your personal and professional development by attending training programs, seeking mentorship, and engaging in continuous learning. As a leader, demonstrate a commitment to growth by actively investing in your own development and encouraging your team to do the same.

By recognizing the importance of personal growth and cultivating the key attributes of a growth profile, individuals can become catalysts for company growth, driving innovation, leading effectively, and achieving sustainable success.

MARKETING AND SALES STRATEGIES

Scaling requires both addition and subtraction.

Sales and marketing funnel

The marketing and sales funnel is often depicted as a simple, linear process that runs from top to bottom, where leads magically trickle down from awareness to purchase due to the force of gravity. This simplistic view can be misleading and detrimental to growth. In reality, a successful funnel requires careful engineering, continuous optimization, and a deep understanding of the customer journey. This chapter delves into the key components of a high-performing funnel, emphasizing the importance of strategic design and data-driven decision-making.

Every marketing and sales funnel has these 4 key components.

1. Reach

- **Targeted outreach:** reach extends beyond mere exposure; it's about effectively reaching the *right* audience. This could involve targeted advertising, strategic partnerships, content marketing, or even direct outreach like cold-calling. The key is to identify the channels and tactics that resonate with your ideal customer profile.
- **Examples:** SEO to attract organic traffic, social media campaigns to engage specific demographics, or attending industry events to connect with potential buyers.

2. Conversion

- **Multi-stage optimization:** conversion is rarely a single-step process. It often involves multiple stages, each requiring careful optimization to guide prospects toward the desired action.
- **Examples:** a landing page optimized for lead capture, a product demo that showcases value, a free trial that encourages engagement, or a compelling sales pitch that closes the deal.

3. Velocity

- **Momentum and efficiency:** velocity emphasizes the importance of maintaining momentum throughout the funnel. Stagnation is the enemy of a successful funnel. The longer a prospect remains in the funnel, the higher the cost and the greater the risk of losing their interest. Efficient processes, timely follow-ups, and streamlined communication are crucial for maintaining velocity.
- **Examples:** automated email sequences to nurture leads, personalized follow-up calls to address questions, or streamlined checkout processes to reduce friction.

4. ROI (Return on Investment)

- **Measuring effectiveness:** every funnel represents an investment of resources—time, money, and effort. Measuring ROI is essential to understand the effectiveness of your marketing and sales efforts. This involves tracking key metrics like Customer Acquisition Cost (CAC), Customer Lifetime Value (CLTV), and conversion rates.
- **Balancing costs and margins:** the cost of sales should be balanced against the company's gross margins. Businesses with high gross margins, like software companies, can often afford higher sales costs due to the profitability of each sale.
- **Examples:** analyzing the cost per lead, calculating the return on ad spend, or assessing the lifetime value of customers acquired through different channels.

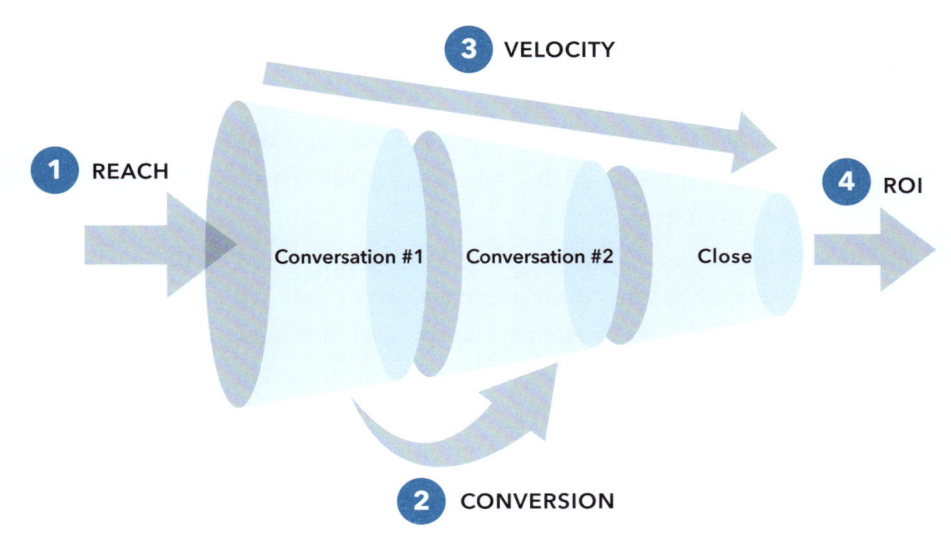

Figure 25 • Key components of marketing and sales funnels

111

Increasing conversion is often easier, cheaper, and more efficient than expanding the reach. First optimize, then expand to get more bang for your buck.

It's important to remember that the overall marketing and sales funnel is an aggregation of multiple funnels operating across different channels and activities. A retail store might have a separate funnel for in-store sales, online sales, and email marketing campaigns. Understanding the performance of each individual funnel contributes to a holistic view of the overall customer journey.

The market and sales funnel is not the end, but the beginning. After the purchase, the focus shifts to **retention**, aiming to retain the customer and build loyalty. Strategies include providing excellent customer support and service, implementing loyalty programs, and maintaining regular updates and engagement with the customer. Finally, in the **advocacy** stage, satisfied customers become advocates, recommending your product or service to others. Encouraging referrals, reviews, and testimonials, and engaging with customers on social media are effective strategies.

The marketing and sales funnel is not a passive conduit; it's a dynamic system that requires careful engineering and continuous optimization. By understanding the key components of reach, conversion, velocity, and ROI, businesses can create a high-performing funnel that effectively converts prospects into loyal, paying customers, driving sustainable growth and profitability.

Deconstructing the funnel: a B2B webinar campaign example

Understanding the dynamics of a marketing and sales funnel is crucial for optimizing lead generation and driving revenue growth. This section deconstructs a B2B webinar campaign funnel, using a visual simulation to illustrate the flow of leads through various stages, the associated costs, and the resulting ROI.

The simulation on p. 115 presents a detailed simulation of a B2B webinar campaign funnel. It showcases the following key elements:

- **Stages:** the funnel is divided into distinct stages, starting with a broad reach (Campaign) and progressively narrowing down to qualified leads (MQL, SQL) and ultimately closed deals (Sales).
- **Conversion rates:** each stage has an associated conversion rate, representing the percentage of leads that move to the next stage. This highlights the importance of optimizing each stage to minimize drop-off and maximize lead progression.
- **Cost per stage:** the simulation also includes the cost incurred at each stage, emphasizing the financial investment required to drive leads through the funnel.
- **Revenue stream:** the final stage (Sales) shows the revenue generated from closed deals, illustrating the financial outcome of the campaign.
- **Overall ROI:** the simulation calculates the overall ROI of the campaign, providing a clear picture of its profitability and effectiveness expressed as a cost of sales.

By analyzing the data presented in the simulation, businesses can gain valuable insights into (1) the efficiency of their lead generation efforts, (2) the overall profitability of the campaign, and (3) the effectiveness of their sales process.

While this simulation provides a valuable example, it's important to remember that every funnel is unique. The specific stages, conversion rates, and costs will vary depending on the industry, target audience, and marketing strategies employed.

By deconstructing this B2B webinar campaign funnel, businesses can gain a deeper understanding of the dynamics that drive successful lead generation and revenue growth.

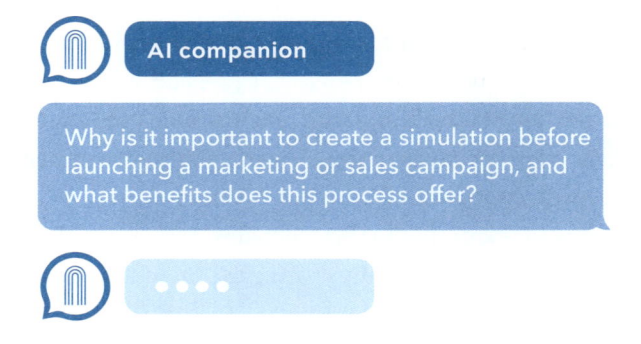

AI companion

Why is it important to create a simulation before launching a marketing or sales campaign, and what benefits does this process offer?

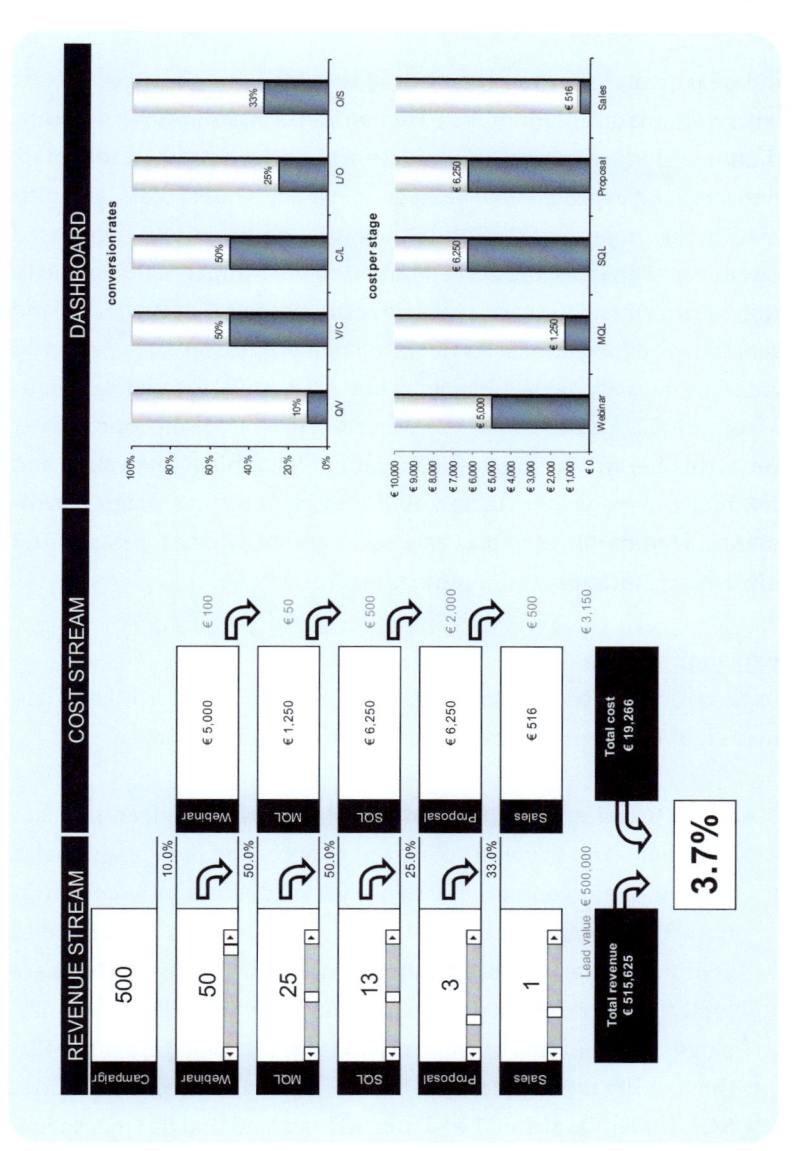

Figure 26 • Simulation of a B2B webinar campaign funnel

Before launching any marketing or sales campaign, it's crucial to start with a simulation, even if it's based on initial assumptions and estimations. This pre-campaign simulation serves as a strategic roadmap, outlining the expected flow of leads, conversion rates, costs, and ultimately, the projected ROI. While the initial numbers might be based on educated guesses, the act of simulating the campaign forces you to think critically about each stage, identify potential bottlenecks, and set realistic expectations. As the campaign progresses and real-world data becomes available, you can refine the simulation, validate your assumptions, and improve the accuracy of your projections. Over time, this iterative process of simulating, launching, analyzing, and refining will hone your team's ability to estimate campaign performance, leading to more accurate simulations, better forecasts, and ultimately, more successful campaigns.

Explanation

In the realm of lead management, MQL and SQL are two key acronyms that represent different stages of lead qualification.

- **MQL (Marketing Qualified Lead):** an MQL is a lead that has shown interest in your products or services and has engaged with your marketing efforts, but is not yet ready for a sales conversation. They might have downloaded a white paper, subscribed to your newsletter, or visited your website multiple times. MQLs are typically nurtured through marketing activities like email campaigns, content marketing, and social media engagement to further qualify them and move them closer to a sales conversation.
- **SQL (Sales Qualified Lead):** an SQL is a lead that has met specific criteria that indicate a higher likelihood of becoming a paying

customer. They have typically progressed further down the marketing funnel, demonstrating a clear need for your product or service, a budget to make a purchase, and the authority to make decisions. SQLs are ready for direct engagement with the sales team, who will then work to further qualify them and ultimately close the deal.

The transition from MQL to SQL is a crucial step in the lead management process, signifying a shift from marketing-led nurturing to sales-led engagement. By effectively qualifying leads and identifying SQLs, businesses can focus their sales efforts on the most promising prospects, improving efficiency and increasing conversion rates.

Deconstructing the funnel: a SEA campaign example

Search Engine Advertising (SEA) is a powerful tool for reaching potential customers online. By placing targeted ads on search engine results pages, businesses can drive traffic to their websites and generate leads. Let's deconstruct a typical SEA campaign funnel, using a visual simulation to illustrate the flow of visitors through various stages, the associated costs, and the resulting ROI.

While this funnel follows a similar overall flow to the previous campaign example, it highlights the unique characteristics of a SEA campaign. The journey begins with a user query on a search engine, representing the initial point of contact. From there, the funnel progresses through various stages: converting the query into a website visit, capturing contact details, qualifying the lead, developing a sales opportunity, and ultimately closing the deal. It's worth noting that the most significant leap often occurs in the first step, converting a search query into a website visit. This highlights the importance of a focus on driving targeted traffic to a website or landing page through relevant keywords and ad copy that capture the user's attention and entice them to click through. Fortunately, SEA mechanisms often operate on a Pay-Per-Click (PPC) model, meaning businesses only incur costs when a user actually clicks on their ad. This cost-effective approach allows for greater budget control and ensures that businesses only pay for genuine expressions of interest.

By analyzing the data presented in the simulation, businesses can gain valuable insights into the effectiveness of their SEA targeting (attracting the right audience), the efficiency of their landing pages and conversion forms (capturing visitor information and generating leads), the overall profitability of the campaign (determining the financial viability of the SEA investment), and the effectiveness of the sales process.

It's important to be aware that SEA campaigns can become more expensive over time. As the popularity of search engine advertising grows and more businesses compete for ad placements, the Cost Per Click (CPC) in bidding systems tends to increase. This means that businesses need to carefully monitor their ad spending and continuously optimize their campaigns to maintain a positive ROI. Strategies for mitigating rising SEA costs include refining keyword targeting, improving ad quality scores, and exploring alternative advertising channels to diversify your online marketing mix.

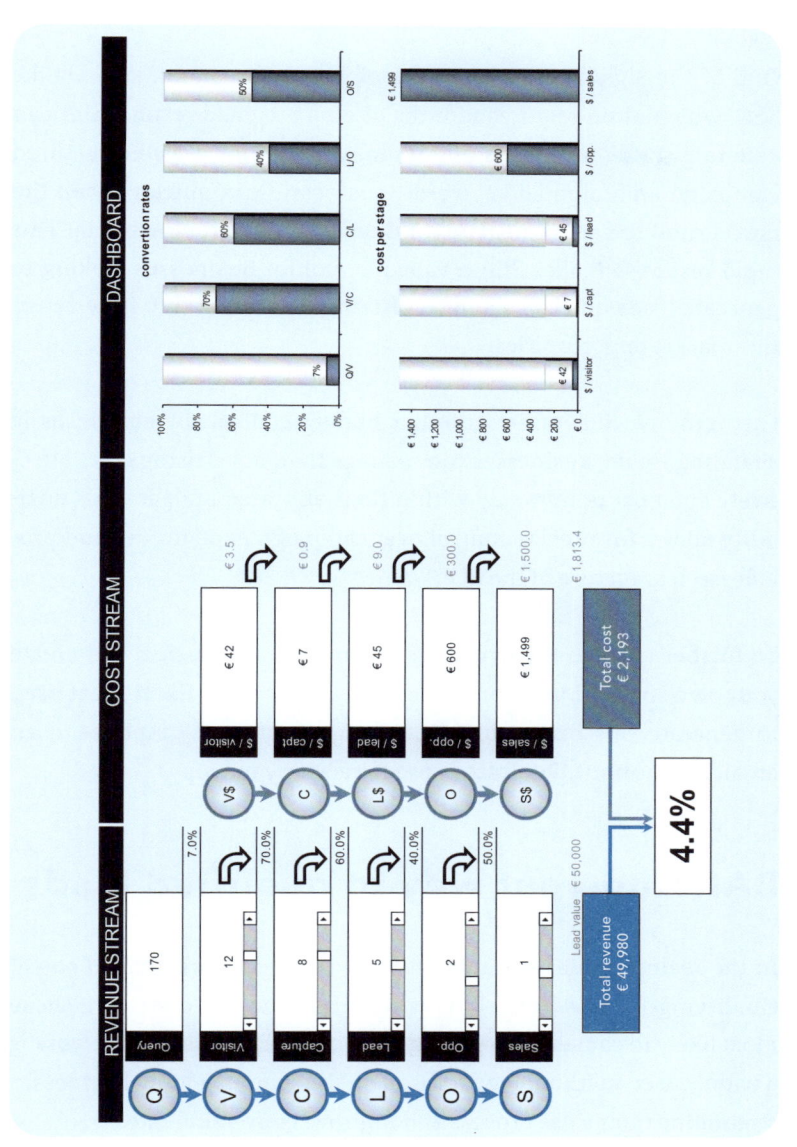

Figure 27 • SEA campaign example

One of the significant advantages of SEA is its immediacy. Unlike SEO, which often requires months of effort to yield results, SEA can generate traffic and leads almost instantly. With a well-structured campaign and targeted keywords, businesses can quickly "open the faucet" and see an immediate influx of visitors to their website. This rapid response makes SEA a valuable tool for businesses looking to generate leads quickly, test new offerings, or respond to time-sensitive market opportunities.

Furthermore, SEA offers granular budget control. By setting daily spending limits, businesses can manage their advertising costs effectively and ensure they stay within their allocated budget. This flexibility allows for precise control over campaign expenditure and provides a clear picture of the ROI.

To further explore the dynamics of funnel optimization and create your own simulations, you can request a copy of the Excel sheet used to generate this B2B webinar campaign example. Simply send an email to **omohout@deloitte.com** to receive your copy.

BANTing your way to qualified leads

In the realm of sales and marketing, not all leads are created equal. Qualifying leads effectively is crucial for focusing efforts on those most likely to convert into paying customers. The BANT framework is a widely used methodology for lead qualification, helping businesses streamline their sales process and improve conversion rates.

BANT is an acronym that stands for:

- **Budget:** does the lead have the financial resources to purchase your product or service?
- **Authority:** does the lead have the decision-making power to make a purchase?
- **Need:** does the lead have a clear need for your product or service?
- **Timeline:** does the lead have a defined timeframe for making a purchase?

In some cases, the BANT framework is extended to BANTS, where the "S" stands for Solution. This addition emphasizes the importance of having a clear and viable solution to the lead's needs before moving forward in the sales process:

- **Solution:** this criterion assesses whether the business has a suitable solution that effectively addresses the lead's specific needs and challenges. It goes beyond simply having a product or service that broadly aligns with the lead's industry or requirements. It involves ensuring that the solution can be tailored or implemented in a way that directly solves the lead's unique pain points and delivers tangible value.

By incorporating the "Solution" criterion into your lead qualification process, you can further refine your sales funnel, focus on high-potential leads, and improve your overall sales performance.

By assessing leads against all these criteria, businesses can identify those that are most qualified and prioritize their sales efforts accordingly.

BANT(S) matters as it can help you focus on high-potential leads, increase downstream conversion rates, and make better sales forecasting. Most important in my experience is that it solves communication problems and misunderstandings between marketing and sales. This "gap" between sales and marketing is a disconnect or misalignment between these two crucial departments within a business. While both teams share the common goal of driving revenue and growth, they often operate in silos, with different priorities, metrics, and communication styles. This misalignment can lead to inefficiencies, missed opportunities, and ultimately, hinder a company's ability to achieve its growth objectives. Sounds familiar, doesn't? This issue gives birth to the RevOps movement—more on that later.

While BANT(S) provides a valuable framework for lead qualification, it's important to adapt its application to the specific context and industry. In some cases, certain criteria might be more or less important than others. For example, in a fast-moving industry, the timeline might be more critical than the budget.

Although BANT(S) is my favorite methodology, it's just one of many lead qualification frameworks available. Other methodologies, such as GPCTBA/C&I (Goals, Plans, Challenges, Timeline, Budget, Authority/Negative Consequences & Positive Implications), provide alternative approaches to assessing lead quality. The choice of framework depends on the specific needs and characteristics of the business and its target market.

Igniting the engines

External growth requires a strategic approach to reaching and engaging your target market. Selecting the right growth engines is crucial for maximizing impact and achieving growth objectives. Consider factors such as your target audience and which channels are most effective for reaching them, which engines best align with your business model and sales process, and whether you have the internal resources and expertise to manage these engines effectively or if you need to partner with external specialists. Also, consider the competitive landscape and which engines your competitors are using, as well as how you can differentiate your approach. Finally, identify potential synergies between different engines and how they can complement each other.

Some growth engines naturally reinforce each other. For example, content marketing can significantly enhance your SEO efforts by providing valuable content that attracts search engine traffic. Similarly, social media can be a powerful tool for amplifying your content marketing and driving engagement. The effectiveness of different growth engines can vary over time and across different markets. It's essential to embrace experimentation, track your results, and adapt your strategy accordingly. Continuously test new approaches, measure their performance, and refine your growth engine mix to maximize your impact.

While some growth engines can be managed effectively in-house, others might require specialized expertise or technology. Consider partnering with external agencies or consultants to leverage their knowledge and resources, especially in areas like SEO, paid advertising, or content creation. Selecting the right growth engines is a critical step in driving external growth. By carefully considering your target audience, business model, and resources, and by embracing experimentation and adaptation, you can ignite the engines that will propel your business toward sustainable success.

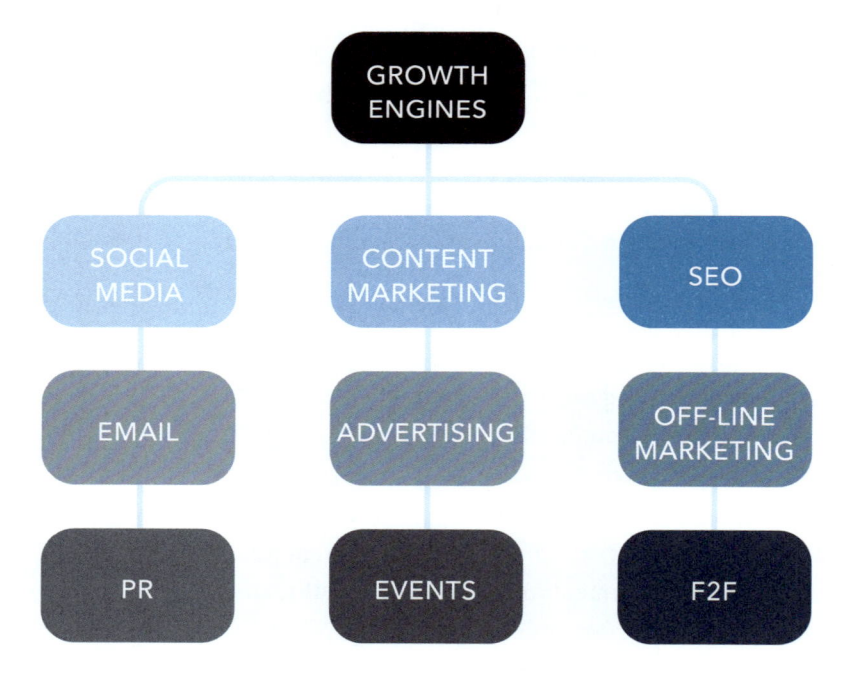

Figure 28 • Growth engines

Companies often prioritize value creation, investing heavily in innovative products and services. However, they should apply the same rigor and creativity to value distribution, encompassing marketing, sales, distribution, and pricing. By doing so, businesses can reach a wider audience, improve conversion rates, enhance customer experience, increase efficiency and profitability, and gain a competitive advantage. This can involve adopting subscription models, establishing direct-to-consumer channels, forming partnerships, personalizing marketing efforts, creating valuable content, and building communities around their brands.

Finding effective growth engines is not a matter of guesswork; it requires a systematic and experimental approach. Start by building a backlog of potential growth engine ideas, drawing inspiration from various sources like industry best practices, competitor analysis, and customer feedback. Treat these ideas as hypotheses that need to be tested and validated.

Experimentation is key. Design experiments with clear objectives, measurable outcomes, and a defined timeframe. Consider factors like your target audience, budget constraints, and the specific metrics you want to track. Launch short sprints, typically lasting two weeks, to test your hypotheses and gather data.

The most likely outcome of your experiment? It might not be successful. But don't view this as a failure; it's a valuable learning opportunity. Analyze the results, identify what didn't work, and use those insights to refine your approach or pivot to a new hypothesis. The ability to learn faster than your competitors is a great competitive advantage. The second most likely outcome is that you discover some value in the tested growth engine. In this case, iterate and refine your approach, launching another sprint to further validate your findings.

How do you become great? Just be good, repeatedly. If the engine continues to show promise and generate a positive ROI, it's time to scale it up and integrate it into your overall growth strategy.

While scaling a successful growth engine, continue to experiment with other ideas from your backlog. This iterative process of testing, learning, and adapting ensures that you are continuously exploring new growth opportunities and optimizing your strategies for maximum impact.

IMPROVING YOUR
EXPERIMENTATION
PROCESS IS WHAT
WILL GET YOU
GROWTH

Mapping your strategy: aligning sales and marketing for external growth

A comprehensive strategy map that effectively visualizes the interconnectedness of various marketing and sales elements to achieve business objectives can be helpful.

The image on p. 128 presents a detailed strategy map that connects various sales and marketing components. It highlights paths to the objectives, which are the central focus of the map, representing the overarching goals and desired outcomes of the sales and marketing efforts.

The map emphasizes the alignment between sales and marketing activities, demonstrating how they work together to achieve common objectives. It illustrates the integration of various marketing channels, including paid, owned, and earned media, to create a cohesive and effective strategy. The inclusion of a "Named Account List" highlights the importance of customer-centricity and building strong relationships with key accounts. Content creation plays a central role in both sales and marketing efforts, feeding into various channels and initiatives. The map implicitly suggests the importance of data and analytics in measuring performance, tracking progress, and optimizing strategies.

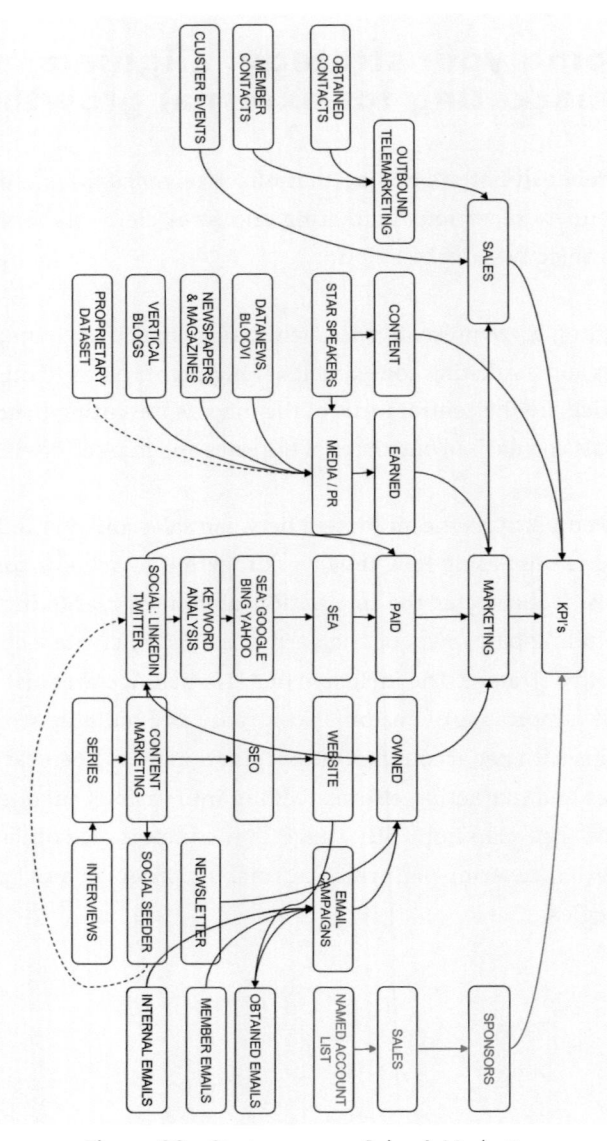

Figure 29 • Strategy map - Sales & Marketing

A strategy map provides clarity and focus, giving a clear visual representation of the overall strategy and helping to align teams and prioritize activities. It also facilitates communication and collaboration between different departments and stakeholders, enables effective tracking of progress toward objectives, and supports data-driven decision-making by providing a holistic view of the sales and marketing landscape.

While this map provides a valuable framework, it's important to adapt it to your specific business needs and objectives. Consider the following: define your objectives, identify your key channels and initiatives, align your sales and marketing efforts, and track your progress and make adjustments. By utilizing a strategy map and embracing a holistic approach to sales and marketing, businesses can create a roadmap for success, driving growth and achieving their business objectives.

The strategy map on p. 130, while comprehensive, also reflects a common reality in business: not all strategies are created equal. In practice, many initiatives will underperform or fail to deliver the expected results. The blue highlighted paths in the image represent the growth engines that truly drive success, while the others may require adjustments, re-evaluation, or even abandonment. This highlights the dynamic nature of strategy, where continuous adaptation and optimization are essential for navigating the ever-changing market landscape and achieving sustainable growth.

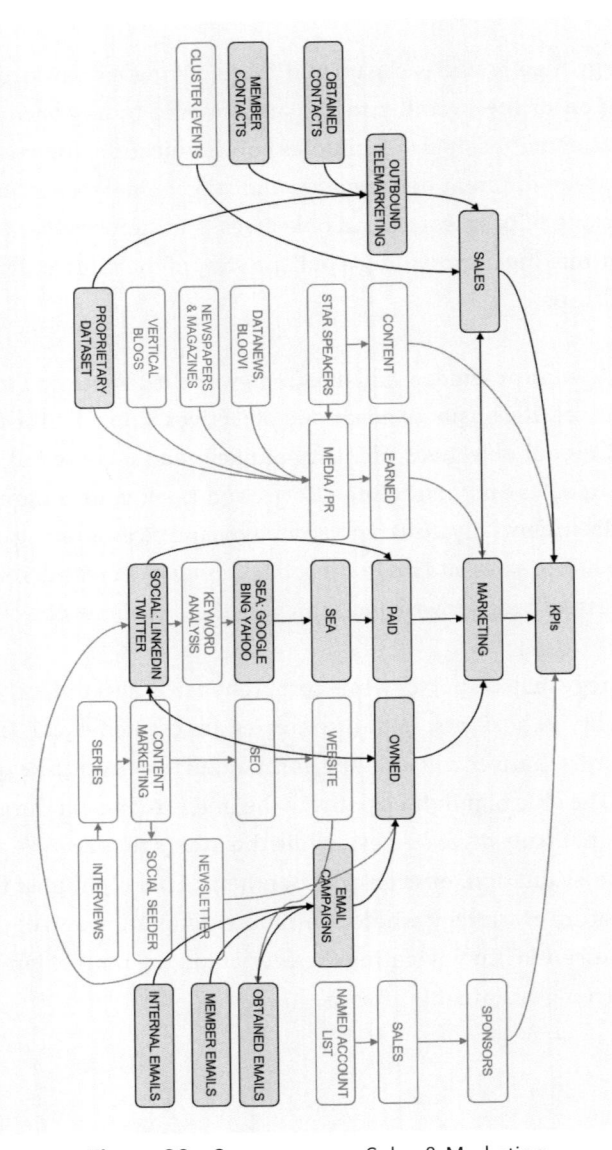

Figure 30 • Strategy map - Sales & Marketing

The power of levers: small changes, big impact

In the pursuit of growth, it's easy to get caught up in searching for grand, sweeping strategies. However, significant growth can often be achieved through incremental improvements in key areas. This section explores the concept of "levers" within a sales pipeline, demonstrating how small changes in various components can compound to create a substantial impact on overall growth.

The image provided on p. 132 illustrates the lever effect in action. It shows how a modest 5% increase in each component of a sales pipeline—the number of leads, the average lead value, and the conversion rate—can result in a remarkable 22% increase in potential sales growth. This highlights the power of focusing on optimizing key levers within the sales process.

The power of levers lies in their compounding effects. Small improvements in each area can multiply to create a significant overall impact. For example, a 5% increase in lead generation, combined with a 5% increase in lead value and a 5% improvement in conversion rate, can result in a much larger overall growth than simply focusing on one area alone.

$$\$ = \frac{(\text{\# LEADS}) * (\$ \text{ LEAD VALUE}) * (\% \text{ CONVERSION RATE})}{(\text{LENGTH OF SALES CYCLE})}$$

$$\downarrow$$

5% INCREASE IN EVERY COMPONENT

$$\frac{(1 + 0.05) * (1 + 0.05) * (1 + 0.05)}{(1 - 0.05)}$$

$$\downarrow$$

22%

POTENTIAL SALES GROWTH

Figure 31 • Lever effect in action

Develop and implement strategies to optimize each lever, such as improving lead generation through targeted marketing campaigns, increasing lead value through upselling and cross-selling, or enhancing conversion rates through sales training and process optimization.

The lever effect demonstrates that significant growth can be achieved through incremental improvements in key areas. By focusing on optimizing the levers within your sales pipeline, you can unlock exponential growth potential and achieve your business objectives. **People who focus exclusively on efforts that matter, succeed. It's that simple.**

RevOps: a holistic approach to revenue growth

In today's complex business landscape, achieving sustainable revenue growth requires more than just a strong sales team or a clever marketing campaign. It demands a holistic approach that aligns all revenue-related functions, from marketing and sales to customer success and finance. That's where the concept of Revenue Operations (RevOps) comes in, a strategy that is transforming how businesses drive revenue growth.

RevOps is a framework that brings together all revenue-related teams—marketing, sales, customer success—under a unified strategy and set of processes. It breaks down silos, fosters collaboration, and leverages data and technology to optimize the entire customer lifecycle, from initial awareness to renewal and expansion.

To effectively implement RevOps, organizations must leverage a range of technologies that enhance collaboration, automation, and data management. It typically requires software in CRM, Marketing Automation, Sales Engagement, and Business Intelligence. In addition, it can be enriched with very specific point solutions such as Hubspot, Aircall (recording calls), and Lusha (finding CEO telephone numbers), etc.

An advanced tool stack can enable superpowers such as:
- **IP targeting:** a method of digital marketing that involves targeting consumers using their IP address and delivering online advertisements accordingly.
- **Geofencing:** creates a virtual geographical boundary that triggers a marketing action to a mobile device when a user enters or exits that boundary.
- **Retargeting:** an online advertising method of reaching out to previous visitors of your website or app, often by displaying ads or sending emails.

Revenue Operations revolutionizes how organizations drive revenue growth by aligning sales, marketing, and customer success functions. Aligned teams close more deals, faster. So basically, RevOps is a new organizational model that drives growth through operational efficiency across the customer lifecycle. To successfully implement RevOps, leveraging the right technologies is crucial. A data platform plays a pivotal role in synchronizing data between SaaS applications, providing a unified view, enhancing operational efficiency, and enabling data-driven decision-making. **Growth strategies consistently fail for one important reason: missing information**. By embracing RevOps and utilizing the right technologies, businesses can unlock their full revenue potential and thrive in today's fast-paced business landscape.

Overcoming sales obstacles

Every sales interaction, regardless of industry or product, faces inherent obstacles. These obstacles, as identified by sales legend Zig Ziglar, represent the key challenges that salespeople must overcome to successfully close deals and build lasting customer relationships. He brings it back to five major obstacles, providing insights and strategies to help sales professionals navigate these hurdles and achieve greater success.

The five sales obstacles

1. **No need:** the customer doesn't perceive a need for your product or service. This could be due to a lack of awareness, a misunderstanding of its benefits, or a belief that their current solution is sufficient.

2. **No trust:** the customer doesn't trust your company, your product, or you as a salesperson. This could stem from a lack of credibility, negative reviews, or a perceived mismatch in values or interests. Also a major issue for startups.

3. **No desire:** the customer might acknowledge a need and trust your solution, but they lack the desire to make a change or invest in your offering. This could be due to inertia, fear of the unknown, or a lack of urgency.

4. **No hurry:** the customer might have a need, trust your solution, and even desire it, but they feel no urgency to make a decision. This could be due to competing priorities, a long decision-making process, or a lack of clear deadlines.

5. **No money:** the customer might have the need, trust, desire, and urgency, but they lack the financial resources to make the purchase. This could be due to budget constraints, competing investments, or a lack of perceived value for the price.

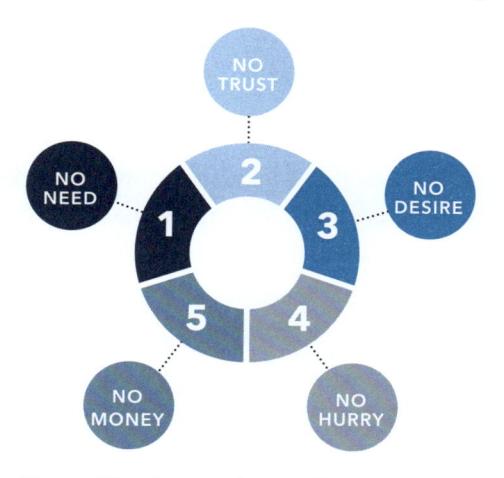

Figure 32 • Overcoming the five sales obstacles

Overcoming these obstacles requires a strategic and adaptable approach. When faced with "No need," the salesperson must educate the customer, clearly demonstrating how their solution addresses specific pain points and provides tangible benefits. If "No trust" is the hurdle, building credibility through expertise, social proof, and genuine rapport becomes paramount. To resolve "No desire," salespeople must paint a compelling picture of the positive outcomes of buying the product and the negative consequences of inaction (= not buying it), creating a sense of urgency. For customers that are in "No hurry," emphasizing time-sensitive offers and potential risks of delay can encourage prompt action. Finally, when "No money" is the obstacle, exploring financing options, demonstrating a strong ROI, and highlighting long-term value can pave the way to a successful sale.

These obstacles are not always independent; they can influence each other. For example, a lack of trust might lead to a decreased perception of need or desire. Addressing one obstacle might require addressing others simultaneously.

While the five sales obstacles model offers valuable insights into common sales challenges, it has faced criticism for oversimplifying the complexities of the sales process. Critics argue that it reduces the intricate dynamics of buyer–seller interactions to five distinct obstacles, neglecting the nuanced interplay between these challenges and other external factors that can influence sales success. Furthermore, the model's lack of context and limited actionability have been highlighted as shortcomings. It doesn't explicitly consider the broader sales environment, such as industry-specific challenges or competitive pressures, and its suggested solutions are often too general to be universally applicable. Another criticism is that the model presents a static view of the sales process, neglecting the dynamic and iterative nature of buyer–seller interactions. In reality, sales interactions are fluid and evolve over time, with obstacles shifting and new challenges emerging as the relationship develops. This static perspective can limit the model's effectiveness in guiding salespeople through the complexities of real-world sales scenarios.

Several alternative sales models offer different perspectives and approaches:

- **Challenger Sale:** emphasizes educating customers and challenging their assumptions.
- **SPIN Selling:** focuses on asking questions to uncover needs and tailor solutions.
- **Solution Selling:** prioritizes understanding customer pain points and positioning offerings as solutions.
- **Consultative Selling:** focuses on building long-term relationships and acting as a trusted advisor.
- **Inbound Selling:** prioritizes attracting customers through valuable content and personalized engagement.

The choice of sales model depends on various factors, including the industry, target market, and company culture. In the past I've used SPIN as it is a good fit for a complex sales cycle with an enterprise focus. For most of the use cases, Zig Ziglar's model is pretty effective.

CASH FLOW, THE LIFEBLOOD OF BUSINESS

Slow down to scale faster—and better— down the road.

Five essential cash flow models

Cash flow is the lifeblood of any business, especially for those focused on growth. It represents the movement of money in and out of the company, and its management is crucial for ensuring financial stability, funding operations, and investing in future growth. This chapter explores various cash flow models, highlighting their impact on business strategy and providing insights into optimizing cash flow for sustainable success. Let's look at this framework of 5 essential cash flow models.

1. Pay now

This model represents immediate payment upon delivery of goods or services. It's excellent for cash flow, as the business receives revenue simultaneously during the transaction. Examples include farmers' markets, traditional software sales (like purchasing a CD with Microsoft Office back in the nineties), and most retail transactions. This model allows businesses to operate without relying on external financing, effectively **bootstrapping customers** for their growth.

2. Pay soon

This model is common in service industries, where payment typically follows the delivery of services, often with a 30- to 60-day delay. To bridge this gap, businesses might rely on bank financing, assuming their customers are creditworthy. In this model, the **bank** effectively **bootstraps** the business by providing short-term credit.

3. Pay first

This is the ideal cash flow model for many businesses. Customers pay upfront when they order, but the business pays its suppliers later, often with a 30- to 60-day delay. This creates a positive cash flow cycle, where the business has access to working capital to fund operations and growth. Examples include supermarkets and e-commerce giants like Amazon and Bol.com or Airbnb. In this model, the **supplier** gets **bootstrapped**.

4. Pay never

This model is often used by businesses that build large user bases or communities. Revenue is generated through sponsorships, advertising, or other means of monetizing the user base. The challenge lies in building a sufficiently large and engaged audience to attract sponsors or generate revenue. Another variation is the open source model. The required scale can vary significantly depending on the business model and target market. And it needs funding too. Hence, in this model, the **investor** is **bootstrapped**.

5. Pay later

This model is common in B2B SaaS companies, where customers pay a recurring subscription fee for access to software. While subscription models offer predictability and recurring revenue, they can create a cash flow challenge, as the business needs to pre-finance the product development and initial delivery. It's similar to a leasing agreement, where the business finances the asset (CapEx) and the customer pays for its use over time (OpEx). Since you are pre-financing this, it's **your business** that is **bootstrapped**.

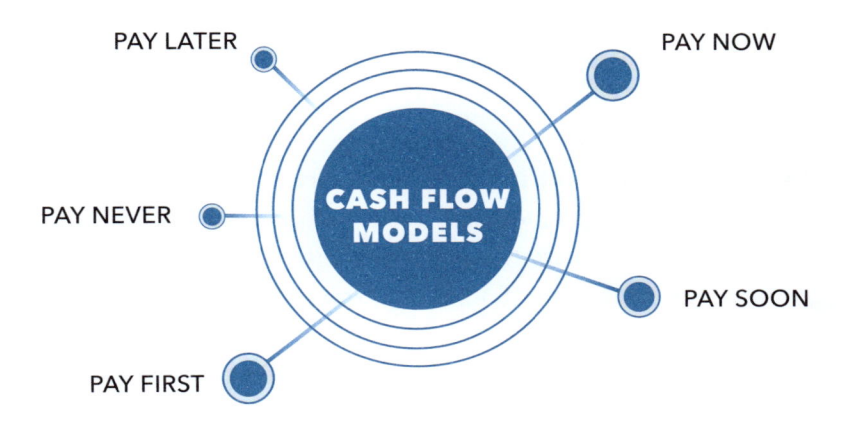

Figure 33 • Cash flow models

Effective cash flow management is crucial for business success. In addition to the cash flow model of your business, it's a domain that needs to be managed actively. Cash flow management is the process of monitoring, analyzing, and optimizing the net amount of cash receipts minus cash expenses. It is essential for ensuring that a business can meet its immediate and short-term obligations. Effective cash flow management involves several key practices.

Firstly, **forecasting** is vital. Regularly projecting cash flow helps businesses anticipate future needs and plan accordingly. This involves creating detailed cash flow forecasts that include all expected cash inflows and outflows. By identifying potential shortfalls in advance, businesses can take proactive measures to mitigate risks.

Invoicing efficiency is another critical aspect. Promptly sending invoices and following up on overdue payments can significantly improve cash flow. Businesses should establish clear credit terms and implement robust accounts receivable processes to ensure timely collection of payments.

Expense management is equally important. Keeping track of expenses and reducing unnecessary costs can help maintain a positive cash flow. This might involve negotiating better terms with suppliers, cutting discretionary spending, or improving operational efficiency.

Working capital management focuses on optimizing the balance between a company's current assets and liabilities. This includes managing inventory levels to avoid overstocking while ensuring there is enough to meet demand. It also involves negotiating favorable payment terms with suppliers and customers to maintain liquidity.

Understanding and managing cash flow is essential for achieving sustainable growth. By carefully considering the implications of different cash flow models and implementing strategies to optimize cash flow, businesses can ensure financial stability, fund their operations, and invest in their future success.

CASH FLOW IS WHERE THE ESSENTIAL PROPERTIES OF A BUSINESS MODEL ARE DETERMINED

Money talks: the language of business

In the world of business, money is the language of communication. To effectively lead and grow a company, leaders need to be fluent in this language, understanding the financial implications of their decisions and how they impact the overall health of the organization. Let's explore the three core financial statements—the Profit and Loss (P&L) statement, the Cash Flow Statement (CFS), and the Balance Sheet (BS)—and how they interact to provide a comprehensive picture of a company's financial performance.

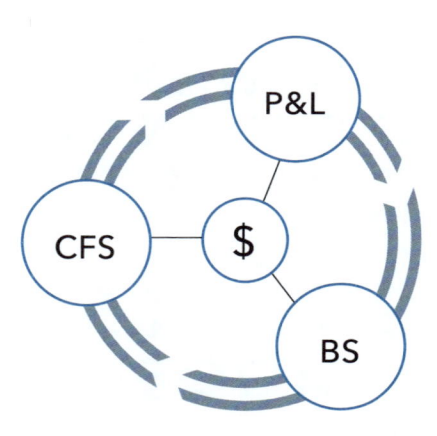

Figure 34 • The financial trinity

The financial trinity

The visual on p. 144 depicts the three financial statements as inter-connected elements revolving around a central dollar sign, symboliz-ing their crucial role in understanding a company's financial health:

- **Profit and Loss (P&L) Statement:** this statement summarizes a company's revenues, costs, and expenses over a specific period, providing a snapshot of its profitability.
- **Cash Flow Statement (CFS):** this statement tracks the move-ment of cash in and out of the company, highlighting its cash generation and usage activities.
- **Balance Sheet (BS):** this statement provides a snapshot of a company's assets, liabilities, and equity at a specific point in time, representing its financial position.

These three statements are not isolated entities; they are dynamically interconnected. Changes in one statement inevitably impact the oth-ers, creating a ripple effect that reflects the overall financial health of the company. For instance, an increase in sales (P&L) might lead to higher cash inflows (CFS) and an increase in assets (BS). Conversely, a significant investment in new equipment (BS) might impact cash flow (CFS) and depreciation expenses (P&L).

Leaders and entrepreneurs don't need to become financial experts, but they do need a solid understanding of how these statements in-teract within their specific industry and company. This knowledge empowers them to:

- **Make informed decisions:** assess the financial implications of strategic choices, such as launching new products, expanding into new markets, or acquiring another company.
- **Monitor performance:** track key financial metrics and identify potential red flags or areas for improvement.
- **Communicate effectively with stakeholders:** articulate the company's financial performance to investors, lenders, and other stakeholders.
- **Drive sustainable growth:** make strategic decisions that support long-term financial health and growth.

To develop financial fluency, you can seek guidance from financial experts, attend financial training programs, and self-study using books or online videos.

Financial literacy is essential for effective leadership and sustainable business growth. By understanding the language of money and the dynamic interplay of the three core financial statements, leaders can make informed decisions, navigate challenges, and steer their companies toward a prosperous future.

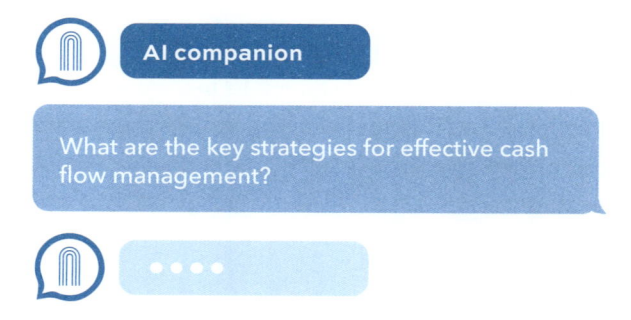

AI companion

What are the key strategies for effective cash flow management?

LESSONS FROM THE DOCTOR'S OFFICE: APPLYING *HOUSE M.D.* TO GROWTH STRATEGIES

Dr. Gregory House, the brilliant but unconventional protagonist of the popular medical drama *House M.D.*, solves perplexing medical cases through keen observation, relentless questioning, and a willingness to challenge assumptions. While his methods might be unorthodox, his approach to diagnosis offers valuable lessons that can be applied to the challenges of growing a business.

1. There are as many diagnostics as there are specialists

Just as there are numerous medical specialties, each with its own diagnostic approach, there are countless perspectives on business growth. Different experts, consultants, and frameworks offer varying solutions and strategies. It's crucial to consider diverse viewpoints, critically evaluate their applicability to your specific situation, and avoid blindly following a single dogma.

2. Everybody lies

"Everybody lies," House often declares. He doesn't blindly accept his patients' accounts; he relies on objective symptoms and evidence. Similarly, in business, it's essential to question assumptions and validate claims. Whether it's a prospect's enthusiastic purchase intentions, a developer's optimistic delivery timeline, or a salesperson's confident sales projections, maintain a healthy dose of skepticism and seek concrete evidence to support their claims.

3. Tests take time, treatment is quicker

"We treat it. If he gets better, I'm right; if he dies, you're right." House's pragmatic approach to treatment reflects the importance of testing and iterating in business. Don't get bogged down in endless analysis and planning. Launch experiments, gather data, and adapt your approach based on real-world results. As Daniel Kahneman suggests in *Thinking, Fast and Slow*, jumping to conclusions can be efficient if the costs of occasional mistakes are acceptable. Embrace a "test and learn" mentality, continuously refining your strategies based on feedback and evidence.

4. Dare to disrupt: challenge the status quo

House constantly questions conventional wisdom and traditional approaches, often defying established medical practices to reach the correct diagnosis. Similarly, in business, a willingness to challenge the status quo, disrupt traditional thinking, and explore unconventional strategies can be crucial for achieving breakthrough growth. Don't be afraid to question "the way things have always been done" and seek innovative solutions that differentiate your business and unlock new opportunities.

5. Fail forward: embrace failure as a learning opportunity

House is not immune to mistakes. His diagnostic process often involves trial and error, and he sometimes pursues incorrect treatments. However, he views these setbacks as learning opportunities, using them to refine his understanding and ultimately arrive at the correct solution. Similarly, in business, setbacks and failures are inevitable. Embrace them as valuable learning experiences, analyze what went wrong, and use those insights to adapt your strategies and improve your chances of future success.

By applying these lessons from the doctor's office, businesses can navigate the complexities of growth with greater clarity, confidence, and a healthy dose of skepticism.

Credit to Bruno Lowagie (founder iText) for the inspirational concept.

Outro

The journey of growth is not for the faint of heart. It's a winding path fraught with challenges, setbacks, and uncertainties. It demands courage, resilience, and a willingness to embrace the unknown. Like Dr. House navigating the labyrinth of medical mysteries, business leaders must confront perplexing challenges, question assumptions, and make difficult choices in the face of incomplete information.

Remember the lessons we have explored together: the delicate balance of external and internal growth, the power of strategic clustering, the art of engineering high-performing funnels, the importance of customer retention, and the need to overcome sales obstacles. These are your tools, your compass, and your guide as you embark on this journey.

Embrace the dynamic nature of growth. The landscape is ever-shifting, demanding agility, adaptability, and a willingness to experiment and learn. Don't be afraid to challenge the status quo, disrupt conventional thinking, and forge your own path. And when faced with setbacks, remember that failure is not an end but an opportunity to learn, adapt, and emerge stronger.

Growth is not a destination; it's a journey of continuous evolution and improvement. It's about pushing boundaries, challenging limitations, and striving for something greater. It's about creating value, not just for your business, but for your customers, your employees, and the world around you.

The path of growth may be arduous, but the rewards are immeasurable. It's a journey of transformation, innovation, and fulfillment. It's a journey that will test your limits, challenge your assumptions, and ultimately, unlock your full potential. So, embrace the challenge, dare to disrupt, and lead your business toward a future of sustainable growth and lasting success. The journey may not be easy, but it will be worth it.

This book itself has been a journey of growth, a testament to the power of collaboration, iterative learning, and a relentless pursuit of knowledge. Now, armed with the insights and frameworks we have explored together, it's your turn. **Go write your own growth story.**

EXPANDING YOUR HORIZONS: RECOMMENDED READING FOR GROWTH

- ***Playing to Win: How Strategy Really Works* by A.G. Lafley and Roger Martin**
  Playing to Win provides a practical framework for strategic decision-making by defining "where to play" and "how to win." It guides readers through choosing their competitive arena and developing a winning strategy. This book is essential for those interested in growth strategies as it offers a roadmap for achieving sustainable competitive advantage.

- ***Profit from the Core: A Return to Growth in Turbulent Times* by Chris Zook and James Allen**
  Profit from the Core advocates for achieving growth by focusing on your core business and existing customers, rather than diversifying. It provides a framework for maximizing core profitability and expanding concentrically. This book is valuable for those seeking sustainable growth strategies, especially in uncertain times, by leveraging existing strengths and customer relationships.

- ***Blitzscaling: The Lightning-Fast Path to Building Massively Valuable Companies* by Reid Hoffman and Chris Yeh**
  Blitzscaling offers a framework for rapidly scaling businesses in winner-takes-all markets. It emphasizes prioritizing speed and market dominance above all else, even at the risk of potential inefficiencies or waste. This book is valuable for those interested in

hypergrowth strategies, providing insights into decision-making, management, and fundraising in a fast-paced environment.

- **SPIN *Selling* by Neil Rackham**
  SPIN Selling provides a research-based approach to sales, focusing on asking the right questions to uncover customer needs and tailor solutions accordingly. It introduces the SPIN framework to guide sales conversations and improve closing rates. Essential reading for those looking to improve their sales effectiveness by understanding customer needs and effectively positioning their solutions.

- **Het *Cashkompas* by Studio Verduyn / Brecht Verduyn (only available in Dutch)**
  A comprehensive guide to financial management for businesses. This book revolves around the central concept of cash and emphasizes its importance as a key indicator of a company's financial health. It is structured around four fundamental questions covering cash flow, assets, profitability, and productivity.

- **Built to Last: *Successful Habits of Visionary Companies* by Jim Collins and Jerry Porras**
  Built to Last explores the characteristics and practices of visionary companies that have achieved enduring success. It identifies key principles such as preserving the core while stimulating progress, building a strong culture, and setting BHAGs. This book is valuable for leaders seeking to create lasting organizations that thrive over the long term by cultivating a strong foundation and pursuing ambitious goals.

ABOUT THE AUTHOR

Omar Mohout is Scaleup Director, M&A and Finance at Deloitte, specialized in helping technology companies fund their growth and get acquired. He has a broad background as a technology entrepreneur, author, C-level advisor, and professor, bringing a wealth of experience and insights to the field. He is deeply involved in the Belgian startup ecosystem, advising and mentoring numerous high-growth companies. His expertise lies in guiding businesses through the complexities of scaling, leveraging technology, and developing effective growth strategies.

Omar is a prolific author and thought leader, having written numerous books on entrepreneurship, digital transformation, and growth strategies. His works include *Pricing Strategies for Startups, 99 Reasons Why Startups Fail*, and *From Idea to Product/Market Fit*. He also shares his insights as a columnist for *Forbes* magazine and contributes to publications like *VentureBeat* and *DataNews*, reaching a wide audience of entrepreneurs and business leaders.

Beyond his writing and advisory roles, Omar is a dedicated mentor and educator. He actively mentors startups and scaleups, conducts workshops, and serves on various boards and committees focused on fostering innovation and entrepreneurship. He is a strong advocate for building a thriving startup ecosystem and actively contributes to initiatives that support the growth of new businesses. His passion for helping businesses succeed is evident in his multifaceted involvement in the entrepreneurial landscape.

He is a sought-after speaker and panelist at leading conferences, sharing his expertise on technology, entrepreneurship, and innovation.

You can contact him via **omohout@deloitte.com.**

ABOUT DELOITTE

Corporate Finance: navigating a world of opportunities

The world of Corporate Finance brings together a diverse range of stakeholders, each with unique perspectives and expertise. From seasoned international investors with targeted portfolios to first-time individual investors seeking to leverage their entrepreneurial success, and strategic industry players seeking strategic or operational investments, the landscape is complex and dynamic.

At Deloitte, our Corporate Finance team serves as your trusted guide through this intricate ecosystem. We help you navigate the spectrum of possibilities and identify the optimal solution tailored to your specific needs. We not only facilitate the identification and engagement of the right investors but also manage every aspect of the process. This includes conducting valuations, designing optimal legal and tax structures, negotiating transactions, and preparing legal documentation—ensuring a seamless and efficient experience for our clients.

With Omar Mohout joining our team, we are significantly enhancing our focus on technology companies. Omar brings an unparalleled network and deep-rooted experience in the Tech sector, which perfectly complements Deloitte's long-standing expertise in Corporate Finance. This powerful combination ensures that Tech entrepreneurs like you benefit from the best of both worlds: deep sector knowledge combined with world-class financial and transactional expertise.

Jan Goemaere | Partner, Deloitte Private | M&A & Finance

Empowering high-scaling companies for a transformative future

As we close this booklet, it's clear that the journey of start/scaleups is about more than growth—it's about transformation. In this context, fostering a vibrant scale-up ecosystem is not just an ambition but a necessity.

Contrary to the common perception that Deloitte primarily serves large enterprises and global players, we made a profound commitment to the startup and scaleup community a few years ago: fostering growth and helping companies realize their full potential through our **Scale-Up Ecosystem Program**.

Built on five key pillars, our approach reflects the depth of our commitment to scaling companies:

Connection: Linking startups and scaleups to our extensive client network, unlocking new markets and opportunities.

Visibility & Recognition: Celebrating growth through programs like the Belgian Fast50, Rising Star, and Most Disruptive Innovator Award, while enabling global benchmarking via the EMEA Fast500.

Collaboration: Partnering with scaleups to co-create, implement, and go to market together, driving mutual growth.

Expertise: Our one-stop-shop approach ensures you are supported every step of the way across critical domains, including Growth strategy; Legal, risk, and compliance; Accounting, tax, and assurance; Technology scalability and security; Funding and liquidity management and; Talent and organization.

Influencing: Shaping a supportive ecosystem through thought leadership, insights, and our upcoming 2025 Confidence Scale-Up Survey Report.

For years now, Deloitte has been at the forefront of the European startup ecosystem: connecting with the brightest minds and most innovative ventures. Yet, what truly sets Deloitte apart is our ability to combine **global scale** with a **multidisciplinary approach**, making us a powerful enabler for scaling companies. By leveraging our robust internal governance, segment-specific expertise, and strong industry partnerships, we bridge the gap between potential and performance, turning ambition into achievement.

Belgium's growth trajectory as a hub for scaling companies is currently in full speed, driven by the collective strength of its ecosystem. At Deloitte, we aim to amplify this momentum, powering the flywheel of innovation, collaboration, and success—now more than ever. The journey of scaling is as inspiring as it is challenging, but it doesn't have to be undertaken alone. **Together, we thrive.**

Anaïs De Boulle | Legal Partner and Scale-Up Leader Deloitte Belgium

LIST OF FIGURES

D/2025/45/194 – ISBN 978 90 209 2291 2 – NUR 800

Academia Press
www.academiapress.be

Academia Press is a subsidiary of Lannoo Publishers.

Omar Mohout
Growth Strategy – The art of scalable growth
Ghent, Academia Press, 2025, 160 p.

Cover and interior design: Gert Degrande | De Witlofcompagnie